# CONT[ENTS]

# ACKNOWLEDGEMENTS

The Authors would like to thank the following people
for their help, support and guidance:
Sunday Mail Editor Jim Cassidy, Brian Steel,
Andrew Sannholm, Ronnie Anderson,
Norman Silvester, Douglas Carr, Tom McGee, Gordon
Birrell and the ever-patient Daily Record and Sunday
Mail library staff.

# PREFACE

THE search for Bible John, Scotland's most elusive killer, has gone on for 28 long, frustrating years. But a bizarre twist in that search came unexpectedly and dramatically. The revelation that police had applied to the procurator fiscal for permission to exhume the body of a man they suspected was a triple sex killer shocked a nation. As it did in the late 1960s and early 1970s, the case again sparked huge public interest, fuelling a new fascination for the Barrowland ballroom killings. Three young women were all murdered after nights out at the dance hall. The sadistic killings of Pat Docker, Mima McDonald and Helen Puttock had striking similarities. Unlike the majority of murder cases the Bible John investigation did not result in a man being charged, brought to court and tried before a jury. In this bizarre case the perpetrator still remains unmasked.

Police hoped advanced forensic science would help them to crack the Helen Puttock case, finally closing the file on the Bible John saga. The astonishing new developments of the first few weeks of 1996 were the catalyst for this book. Many times during the project we thought back to the long hours hundreds of dedicated police officers endured during the height of the original inquiry. That amazingly detailed police investigation provided a wealth of information and background material which, coupled with our own research, helped  to get this book on the shelves to tell for the first time, the up-to-date story of the continuing riddle of Bible John - Scotland's most puzzling murder mystery ever.


Alan Crow and Peter Samson
Glasgow, January, 1997.

# CHAPTER ONE

## THE GRAVE'S SECRET

*"Can any hide himself in secret places, that I shall not see him, saith the Lord."*
Jeremiah 23:24

THE grey, icy, early morning calm was shattered at 9.07 on February 1, 1996. From the white marquee erected just an hour earlier came the clattering of pneumatic drills, biting and driving into the solid, frozen ground.

A portable generator, parked just outside the open flap on one side of the marquee, droned away feeding power to the drill blades. The only other sound was the distant buzz of motorway traffic on the M74 linking Scotland with England.

A blonde woman wrapped against the bitter cold in a beige, dark fur-trimmed coat stood patiently waiting. She constantly shifted from one foot to the other, rubbing her hands to keep warm. Green Wellington boots protected her feet from the blanket of snow.

Uniformed policemen stood close by surveying the scene, an officer standing guard at the gate of the isolated walled graveyard in the heart of Scotland. New police recruit, 23-year-old Dawn Ogilvie nervously guarded the tent. It was only her first week in the job. A trio of plain-clothed officers arrived in a green Peugeot, parking on the single track outside. Bracing themselves against the biting wind, they made their way directly through the tombstone maze and went into the marquee, re-appearing minutes later to chat to the blonde figure waiting just outside. At her feet stood a small rectangular case.

A blue truck, proudly displaying a Royal warrant for supplying the Queen with marquees and tents, had arrived at the cemetery just before 7.30am. Normally the firm set up marquees for weddings or garden parties. But today they were there for a very different reason. In the chilly darkness just before dawn and battling against a keen frost, the small team of men busily worked away setting up the marquee's metal framework before draping it with thick white, plastic-coated canvas.

One of the workers stood back when the job was completed, proudly surveying his team's work. Minutes later the blue truck drove out through the huge rusty iron gates as yet another team of police officers drove in.

About half a dozen graves were hidden behind the white shroud-like walls of the marquee. The small group of people who had moved inside focused their eyes on just one.

The area had been carefully measured out. Light-coloured tape lay on the ground, marking out the key area. The details of who was buried where had been painstakingly checked and double-checked with local council officials.

Before the the marquee's final flap was drawn to block out prying eyes, a team of pressmen fixed their sights on that same tombstone.

THE NAME ON THAT HEADSTONE WAS JOHN IRVINE McINNES - THE MAN POLICE BELIEVED TO BE BIBLE JOHN.

He'd been buried there in 1980 after taking his own life by slashing a main artery under his armpit. McInnes had taken his secrets to that grave. Was he a monster who preyed on young women? Did his sadistic reign as Bible John bring fear to a generation of fun-loving women, all frighteningly aware that a night out at the dancing could end in death?

His remains were about to be exhumed from his resting place in the grave he shared with other members of his family. That dawn exhumation would hopefully give police the last missing pieces in a jigsaw. They hoped those final clues would be found, allowing them to close the files on a mystery that gripped a nation in the late 1960's and had remained unsolved for almost 30 years.

Over the next few months, using the latest forensic knowledge and crime-busting technology, police experts analysed samples from McInnes' remains. They hoped DNA tests, the genetic fingerprints used to trap murderers and rapists, would positively link McInnes to the 1969 murder of Helen Puttock - the killing that spawned the nickname Bible John. She, like two other young women - Pat Docker and Mima McDonald - had been murdered after a night out at Glasgow's legendary Barrowland ballroom.

The police officers suddenly stopped digging and drilling as they caught the first glimpse of a coffin. That was the signal for the experts to move in. Carefully and painstakingly they set about the first task of exhuming the body of McInnes' mother, Elizabeth. A local undertaker stood by with a coffin to transport her remains to his funeral parlour. She'd died an old woman - 91 years of age - and was buried seven years after her son. Locals were horrified at the prospect of her remains being disturbed. McInnes' father Robert was first to be buried in the lair, aged 60, back in September, 1954.

Just after 10.30am Elizabeth McInnes' remains were carefully placed in the fresh coffin. Lime was used to kill any bacteria. Mrs McInnes' remains were driven away in a black Volvo estate, to be re-interred during a short funeral service at a later date.

Attention then turned to the next part of the proceedings. This was the most crucial part of the excavation. A second hearse and another coffin, an outsize model, was summoned to the cemetery. This time police believed the vehicle's cargo was a killer - a man hunted by detectives for more than a quarter of a century.

Shortly before noon the digging crew touched the coffin containing John McInnes. Metal sheets and scaffolding were used to shore up the crumbling walls of the grave. The men involved in the task were protected by white or black overalls and masks. The sweat on their brows and backs froze when they stopped for a break from the macabre task. They braved the cold but such was the intensity of the sub-zero climate that portable gas heaters had to be brought in. The destination of the second hearse was the main police mortuary in Glasgow, located in the Saltmarket area in the city centre.

Within hours McInnes' body was laid out on a cold steel mortuary table - an amazing 16 years after his death - his secrets ready to be disclosed.

# CHAPTER TWO

## AN ANGEL'S DATE WITH SATAN

*"Her sun is gone down while it was yet day..."*
Jeremiah 15:9

PRETTY Pat Docker was an angel. She enjoyed her job as a nursing auxiliary, helping the hospital medical staff and caring for the patients as best she could. She worked night shift from 10pm to 8am with her days off on Tuesdays, Wednesdays and Thursdays. The system suited her well. It also fitted in with domestic arrangements. She effectively job-shared with her mother who worked the three midweek nights at the hospital. Between them they cared for Pat's four-year-old son, Sandy. She never needed a baby-sitter. Living at home with her parents in Langside Place, Battlefield, Glasgow, meant Pat's wee boy always had company. He was always content - as long as there was a familiar face, someone to chat to him, make him laugh, play with him, feed him and put him to bed, he rarely complained.

Twenty-five-year-old Pat's attractive looks turned heads. She was about five foot three inches tall and had dark-brown wavy hair, cut short and hazel eyes. She had a tip-tilted nose.

She was married but at the time - five years after her wedding - was living apart from her RAF corporal husband Alex, 25, who was based in Lincolnshire. The couple had spent some time together while he was serving in Cyprus but in the previous May, Pat and their son had returned to Glasgow and moved into her parents' flat. The pair had been there for about a year. The subject of a divorce had been raised but neither side had proceeded further. Life for Pat was her part-time job at Mearnskirk Hospital, looking after her son . . . and the dancing!

She enjoyed escaping from her parents' home to relax. Her parents didn't have a problem about her going out on the town. They knew, that at 25, her life needed a bit more excitement and they were always happy to help out on the baby-sitting front. On Thursday, February 22, 1968, Pat made up her mind to go to the dancing. She cleared it with her parents - little Sandy was always uppermost in her thoughts - and told them she was going to the city's Majestic Ballroom. She liked it there and knew some of the regulars and was happy to dance with some of the men who frequented the popular haunt. But she didn't go there. Strangely she changed her mind and, instead, headed to the Barrowland Ballroom. That decision - now impossible to explain - was to prove fatal.

Dancing and football were the great Glasgow pastimes, with the former perhaps just shading the latter in the popularity stakes. The city boasted great dance halls - The Albert, the Majestic, the Plaza and the Locarno. Dancing or jiggin' had really gripped the city in the early 1930s. The Barrowland, in Glasgow's Gallowgate, opened in 1934 and soon became the city's most popular ballroom. It was the "in" place and no stranger to controversy.

One incident attracting press coverage was billed as a "Dust-up in the powder room" . . .

The steel-tipped stiletto came crashing down on the young girl's head. She screamed in agony as blood poured from her wound, splashing her flimsy gold-coloured evening dress. It was just another row in the ladies' toilet at the Barrowland dance hall. A teenager was arguing with another girl when a woman stepped in to try and break it up. Suddenly the teenager screamed in agony - hit over the head with the shoe. She later needed two stitches in her head. Another girl who was caught up in the cat-fight needed seven. It was a fight like hundreds of others before it, but this one made the newspapers. It was the mid-1960s and the girl wielding the stiletto was only 17. The row landed her in court. She pleaded guilty to two charges of assault. "You are very fortunate that I am not sending you to prison," said the Sheriff. He placed her on probation for two years.

The original ballroom on the site was opened by Mrs Maggie McIver, known as the queen of the Glasgow Barrows - or Barras - the name given to the nearby market stalls area. It was destroyed by fire in August 1958, but restored and reopened two years later by the family in the best McIver tradition. During World War Two, the Barrowland was a mecca for visiting servicemen - Yanks, Canadians, Poles, Norwegians. You name it, they all managed to find their way to the East End of Glasgow, and that dance hall. Even after the war the popularity continued over the next two decades with Billy MacGregor and his Gaybirds, the resident band. They were a 16-piece orchestra, although their numbers were often depleted because some members of the band had one too many in the pubs on the way to the Barrowland. Other famous band leaders such as Henry Hall, Roy Fox, Teddy Joyce and Jack Hylton travelled to the city to conduct and delight the dancing crowds.

Barrowland - or Barraland as the natives pronounced it - struck just the right mix of 20-35 year-olds. Factory girls who worked in the now upmarket Merchant City daydreamed in the sewing machine sweat shops and at cutting tables wishing the hours away for their all-important Friday night date at their favourite ballroom. On a Friday evening they could be seen going home, their heads wrapped in curlers, covered over with a colourful turban fashioned from a head scarf. A quick tea and wash-up. Out came the rollers and the remaining frizz was tortured into the hairstyle of the day as they prepared to meet their dream partner.

Those seamstresses and tailoresses unlucky enough to work late on Fridays took their frocks and dancing pumps to work in their message bags. A fish supper sufficed, then onto the dancing and they would emerge from the ladies toilets "sans" curlers and overalls ready for a night's entertainment. Glasgow Corporation bus conductresses were known to arrive in full uniform, minus money bag, with their dance finery hidden in a huge holdall ready for the transformation. Parts of the ballroom had names like Geordie's Byre, Johnnie Scobie's Bar and The Lumber Room. The ballroom was well policed with polite but firm attendants. Soft drinks could be had from a bar, but alcohol was strictly taboo. However no respectable girl ever arrived without a "cairry-oot"- possibly a half bottle of vodka - in her handbag to quietly pass around her chums as a "mixer" for their soft drinks. It was all done out of sight of the attendants.

In the 1950s, Glasgow was overrun with razor thugs. Many a young man was scarred for life in the back streets - his only crime to innocently chat up some hard man's girl in the ballroom. The proximity of Glasgow

Green provided a haven for new-found romance partners from the ballroom. After the last dance amorous pairs made their way to the sprawling park for an hour or so before rushing back up to main streets for the tram or - cash allowing - a taxi home.

The heyday of the Barrowland was the 1940s and 1950s. The 1940s ushered in the big time, good time party atmosphere when visiting allied servicemen homed in on the ballroom to chat up the war "widows" missing their husbands and boyfriends who were "somewhere in France fighting for King and country". Money was plentiful then with full employment for the girls in the city and GIs with pockets filled with dollar bills, condoms and nylons. Many children were born out of wedlock in these years and the foreigners shouldered much of the blame. One Glasgow man born in 1944 and abandoned by his mother soon after birth believed his love for Western movies and the great American prairies was the result of his mother's fling with a US serviceman she met at the Barrowland. He was certain his dad was a ranch-hand named Hank who had a six-month relationship with his mother. He discovered all this years later after tracing his family, and although his mother had died his new-found aunt filled him in on the background.

The Ballroom remained a popular venue in the 1950s, although losing some of its glamour with less money around and a change of clientele. Men and women cheating on their partners chose the Barrowland for stolen nights of fun and passion. Many a married woman told her stay-at-home husband she was just popping round to a girlfriend's house for a few hours. The uninterested husband failed to notice as she smuggled a large carrier bag out the front door. Inside she'd stashed make-up, dress and dancing shoes. More than once did cheating couples bump into each other at the Barrowland with catastrophic results.

Rock 'n' roll arrived in the early 1960s sending The Gaybirds into the annals of musical memories. It was not unusual to see scenes of 1500 screaming hysterical teenagers pushing, jostling and trying to invade the rostrum where the star of the day was appearing. The Barrowland was a big attraction in a city that at one point had the most dance halls per head of population in the UK. And it proved to be a great attraction for John McInnes.

Thursdays were different at the Barrowland. It was considered to be a "secret" night when the over-25s who turned out preferred not to reveal their whereabouts. It wasn't a sordid sex den - more a venue for illicit get-togethers for married men or women.

On that Thursday there was a carnival night - a special laid on by the management. The music was different. The atmosphere was fuelled by the excitement of many of the dancers who knew full well they were in the wrong. They were cheating on their partners but loving every minute of it. Men and women at the Barrowland on Thursday nights didn't always reveal their true identities, using false names. It was all part of the cheating game. Why Pat chose to tell her parents she was going to the Majestic and then go elsewhere remains a mystery. In the early days after her death, Pat's lie confused, angered and added to their grief. It also hampered the police inquiry. It was a lie that helped her killer escape justice.

When Pat was enjoying her dance hall days the music scene was buzzing. The Beatles had headed off to India and were seen meditating at the Maharishi Yogi's spiritual centre on the shores of the sacred River Ganges. Scots singing sensation Lulu was promoting a new line of clothes - a white crepe dress and a sleeveless navy maxi-coat, together costing just under £9. More generally girls' talk centred around news that the Queen's doctor was advocating that the contraceptive pill should be available on the National Health Service. That could signal a big change in the social scene, the girls - and boys - agreed. Talk among the country's smokers was that cigarette prices were going up. A packet of 20 cost around five shillings (25p). A ban on buying Rhodesian tobacco was blamed for the expected price hike. Scotland's publicans were asked if they wanted to open on Sundays. The Vietnam War raged on and the Prime Minister, Harold Wilson, was jeered as he toured South Wales. The new decimal coins had just been unveiled - ready for the 1971 switch – and TV highlights were the Rolf Harris Show, The Man from U.N.C.L.E. and coverage of the Winter Olympics from Grenoble, France. A new magazine was launched - called 19 - and the first edition featured an article on "Fashionable looks for girls who go places". It was billed as "gorgeously glossy, daring and different" all aimed at capturing the 18-25 female market.

That night Pat Docker was going places. She left the house in a yellow crocheted mini dress - quite the fashion in those days. It was still winter and the weather was bitterly cold. She topped her outfit with a grey duffel coat with a blue furry collar and wore brown shoes. She lifted her brown handbag as she left the flat, and the hall light flashed on her grandmother's wedding ring which she wore on her right hand. Her bright smile lit up her face. She was a young, slim, very attractive woman in the prime of life.

When she arrived at the Barrowland, Pat headed to the ladies room. She did a quick once-over check - hair, make-up and clothes, took a deep breath and headed out into the crowd which had built up even in the few minutes she'd been gone. A quick visit to the bar, glass charged and Pat picked a spot overlooking the dance floor. It was always important to find a good vantage point - not just to see but to be seen. There's no point being on the shelf if you don't push yourself to the edge to be dusted down from time to time.

Pat stood there, drink in hand, surveying the dance floor. She saw a man standing to her right-hand side. She paid little attention to him. Then he was at her left. He smiled. She smiled back. Then another of the dancing crowd came from the floor in her direction and gently pushed into her. Pat lost her footing slightly and bumped into that smiling man. They both apologised at the same time and laughed. He was going to feature in her life for the next few hours. He was polite and taken by her good looks, smile and personality. He was the man who would take her life. He was her killer.

The next morning joiner Maurice Goodman set out from his home to his lockup garage around the corner. He lived near Pat's parents. He kept his car in the garage and as he reached the door, keys at the ready, he spotted something in a recess. It looked like a body. He was shocked. It was a woman, naked, lying crumpled like a large half-empty flour sack. The body had been there for hours, slumped and frozen in the February cold. Her head lay to the one side. A used sanitary towel was discovered nearby. It was Pat's. She had been menstruating at the time of her death - a feature that linked her to the killer who was later to be known as Bible John.

Nurse Pat had been murdered. She'd been strangled with her tights and her face and head were badly beaten, probably kicked and punched. All her clothing was missing, except for her brown shoes. Police launched a murder probe. During door-to-door inquiries they traced a woman who claimed she'd heard a woman shout out as if in distress. She'd shouted "Let me go" or "Leave me alone" or both. It was a voice pleading for help, urging someone, somewhere to come to her rescue. In the end the man silenced her before leaving her alone, dead.

For some time the police didn't know the victim's identity. The evening newspapers ran the story of the naked woman and the police murder inquiry. It was then, as the publicity machine moved into top gear, that Pat's dad John Wilson started to fear the worst. She hadn't come home after the dancing but she often stayed with one of her girlfriends. On the Friday evening he started to feel uncomfortable. The penny was dropping. The body had been discovered about 200 yards from his home. The body was his daughter's.

Pat's estranged husband was high on the suspect list but only because the police were keeping all options open. He'd been on leave at the time of her murder but was staying at his parents' home in East Lothian. They confirmed he'd been there with them on the evening of the murder and had travelled to St Andrews the following day. Further inquiries were made and he was tracked down in the world-famous golfing town and told of the horror. He was anxious to help with the inquiry but could tell detectives little about his wife's comings and goings. He told police he hadn't seen her for about five months or so. He was driven to Glasgow to complete the identification of his wife's body. The murder hunt was stepped up. A thousand special posters were printed and a plea was made for information about the driver of a Morris 1000 Traveller which had stopped at a nearby bus stop late on the night of the murder. A massive reconstruction of what were believed to be Pat's last movements was staged. A search of the nearby River Cart revealed little - the casing for her watch and eventually her handbag, but these items were of little help to the police.

A mock-up picture was released using a policewoman in the same type of clothing Pat wore on the night she died. Less than a month later the police announced they were seeking a man with bruised or cut knuckles. Hundreds of taxi drivers were quizzed in an effort to establish how Pat had travelled home. They hoped someone would remember if she'd travelled with a man - the man they wanted to quiz over her death.

An anonymous letter was sent to the police, its author hinting that she possibly knew the identity of the killer. A group of journalists - reporters and photographers - had been at a party hosted by a newspaper man in his home near the murder scene. They were quizzed to establish if they'd seen or heard anything. Some fell foul of their news editors who reckoned they'd been partying when they should have been doing their jobs, looking for stories.

What turned out to be one of Scotland's biggest ever murder stories had happened just a few dozen yards from the partying press pack . . .

Was this the first taste of blood for the man who was to become a triple killer? Did Pat Docker die at the hands of Bible John?

# CHAPTER THREE

## MIMA'S LAST WALTZ

*"Suffer the little children to come unto me...."*
Mark 10:14

THREE little, innocent children played in the mid-August sun. They didn't have a care in the world. And that was exactly how the picture should have stayed. They spent hours in the streets and the back courts, running up and down the closes shouting and screaming. Toys weren't important. They were too expensive for mum's purse anyway. She needed to keep her eye on the priorities. Mum had to think about back-to-school purchases - a school bag could be picked up for five shillings (25p), a boy's shirt for ten shillings (50p) and a girl's blouse for eleven (55p), but when you added up the cost to kit out three youngsters it was a fair sum. These children had put all thoughts about returning to school well to the back of their minds. It was still the holidays.

They were happy, they had each other and their wild imaginations fuelled daft ideas for games, chasing here, there and everywhere. They had their gangs of friends, youngsters from the same class or school who they'd meet up with to pass the holidays. They were used to mum being out - they didn't care that much because aunt Margaret was always on hand to look after them. But in an hour their lives changed, shattered by a short phrase, gently uttered by a police officer. That one sentence said it all - *"Your mummy's dead."*

The trio - Elizabeth, 12, Andrew, nine, and seven-year-old Alan - were the McDonald kids from Mackeith Street, Bridgeton in Glasgow. They were immediately taken into the care of a local authority home. The body of their mum Jemima - known as Mima to her pals and close family - had been found in a derelict ground-floor flat just yards from their own tenement. The 32-year-old, five feet seven inches tall, slim-built with shoulder-length dark brown hair, was wearing a black pinafore dress with a white frilly blouse and sling-back high heeled shoes. On Saturday, August 16, 1969, she'd gone out to the dancing. To the Barrowland. But she didn't make it home.

She was found beaten, partly-clothed and strangled with her own tights. Detectives discovered she'd been menstruating. Despite an extensive search - even through dustbins - her handbag was never found. Post-mortem results revealed she'd been lying there for about 30 hours. Police believed Mima left the Barrowland with the man who killed her. They were sure she'd probably danced the last waltz with him. Minutes after midnight she'd agreed to let her dance partner see her home . . .

Mima McDonald, separated from her husband, loved her nights out on the town. She liked to dance - the hits of the day were music to her ears and she'd happily spend hours swinging her hips in time to the beat. She looked forward to her visits to the Barrowland - she viewed that dance hall as her "local" - and would put on her best gear and head there on Thursdays and, especially, the more popular Saturday nights. These visits were like some sort of drug - she could let her mind escape from the pressures of being a mother with a young, demanding family. She could enter a world of high living, enjoy a touch of glamour and a buzz that would keep her going through the rest of the week. Once there she'd see the usual faces, the regulars who she'd danced alongside on so many occasions. But it was always refreshing to see a fresh face, someone new on their first visit. She always kept an eye open for that handsome face in the crowd. A well-turned out young man, hair slicked back, and sporting a sharp suit that looked as if it had just come out the tailor's shop. Looks and that first impression were all so important.

She didn't really have a problem if she wanted to go out for the evening. She had the children to think about but she was fortunate. She had a baby-sitter on her doorstep - next door in fact.

The McDonalds lived in a tenement block - it wasn't the best place in the city to be living in but Mima had made it as comfortable as she could. The children's father no longer featured in her life. But right across the landing lived her sister Margaret O'Brien. It was a convenient situation and Margaret regularly helped out with the children while Mima was out. Few if any of her pals could boast of a baby-sitter who was so handy. She had to be careful not to abuse that fact.

The summer of 1969 had seen the Ulster crisis deepen. It was a hot spell of weather. A baby died from heat-stroke after being left in a parked car. Football hero George Best was snapped with a 20-year-old blonde Danish model. The world's longest-surviving heart swap patient died in Cape Town more than 19 months after the transplant.

Z Cars and the Mike and Bernie Show were peak-time TV shows but with the pleasant, balmy evenings few were staying indoors to watch.

On that August night Mima got dressed up, throwing on a brown woollen coat with a belt. It could get slightly cooler later at night and there was no point getting a chill after leaving the hot, steamy atmosphere of the dance hall, she thought. She also wore a head scarf and carried a simulated leather handbag. Under the scarf she hid a little secret . . . she kept her rollers in her dyed hair. It was a trick of the trade shared by many of the other dancing girls. Mima spent as much time as she could perched in front of the mirror ensuring the rollers were tightly secured in place. But the way to improve the style's longevity was simple. Keep the rollers in right up until the last possible moment. It was the next best thing to looking as if you'd just stepped out of the hairdresser's salon. Don't forget that first impression, she remembered.

On arrival at the Barrowland Mima's first destination was the ladies' room. Off with the coat, the head scarf and a quick twirl in front of the mirror to check everything was just right. All OK. Then the final hair session was underway. The pins were removed, the rollers twisted out and stuffed into the handbag and the hair was ready for dancing! A final check on the make-up, a last roll-over with her lipstick and she was prepared to step out from the protection of the ladies' room on to the dance floor. She'd done it many times before and it always worked.

Mima was a familiar face in the Barrowland and a number of people that night remembered seeing her. They'd nodded, smiled and some had chatted as she mingled and weaved through the crowds. After midnight she'd left with a man, the guy she'd danced the last waltz with after he'd chatted her up. A girl later spoke of how she'd seen Mima sitting on a settee at the

Barrowland. That was normally where the suitor would coax his girl to in the hope of getting a cuddle, a kiss and a fumble.

Mima's chosen partner for that night was aged between 25 and 35, tall with reddish-fair hair, cut short. He was smartly dressed in a well-cut suit and a gleaming white shirt. He had the appearance of being particular - or with a mother who wouldn't let him out looking anything but his best. The pair had chatted - Mima mentioning in the passing that she had three youngsters but not making a big thing about it. She didn't really want to put him off too soon. They'd only just met. He quietly listened throwing in a few, scant facts about his own life. He was polite and clearly-spoken but guarded about his identity and background. Mima gave most away, but she was relaxed, happy to have company and confident that on this occasion she'd not be walking home alone. It was a good night out. So far.

After the final note of that last waltz, Mima made a quick dash to the ladies' room and checked her appearance. The hair was OK and the lips were still looking good. She put on her coat, leaving the belt loose and headed out to team up with her partner. They stepped outside into the mild early morning air and started strolling homewards.

From the Barrowland they headed into Bain Street then into London Road and on to Bridgeton Cross. Witnesses spoke of seeing the pair together. That walk - eventually bringing them into Mackeith Street - was less than a mile. Walking slowly it should have taken no more than half an hour. The pair headed into that dirty, deserted tenement building - an ideal spot for a quiet session of kissing, cuddling and heavy petting. But Mima's man had a different kind of lust - a passion for

29

killing. Mima was raped and strangled with her own tights. The killer coldly walked away from that horror scene, leaving Mima's lifeless frame.

The following day no-one really missed Mima. It wasn't entirely out of the ordinary for her not to come home. But her sister Margaret just went about her usual job of getting the kids up and organised. For them it was just another day for playing outside. They'd slept well and recharged the batteries ready for action. It was one day nearer back to school so there was no time to waste. Soon, however, Margaret did start worrying. The hours crept by and she was concerned. She overheard some other kids from the street chattering on about something being discovered in a nearby derelict building. The youngsters referred to "the body". They sounded excited. But Margaret O'Brien realised there could be something dreadfully wrong. She headed to the building to find out for herself. She found her sister, dead, dumped and deserted in a bed-recess. Margaret was appalled, in a state of shock and heartbroken. Her sister's night out at the dancing had cost her the ultimate price. The body's temporary crypt had once been a home for a family. From that moment on it would always be known as the house where Mima McDonald was murdered.

Mima's distraught family clubbed together, gathering up what money they could to put up a £100 reward. It was a handsome enough sum at that time but not even that bait was enough to hook someone with the vital clue to lead police to the killer.

A week after she died the police staged a public reconstruction of her final known movements. A policewoman who bore a resemblance to the tragic mum dressed in similar clothes and walked the death route from the ballroom to Mima's home street. The detective leading the hunt knew there had been a number of people around at the time Mima and her man walked home on that fateful, early morning. The reconstruction threw up some new information, but not enough.

The killer was on the loose. Police believed Mima and Pat Docker were victims of the same monster....*and the Barrowland was his hunting ground.*

# CHAPTER FOUR

## DANCING WITH THE DEVIL

*"And when she could no longer hide him, she took for him an ark of bulrushes, and daubed it with slime and with pitch, and put the child therein; and she laid it in the flags by the river's bank; and his sister stood afar off, to wait what would be done to him."*
Exodus 2:3-4

HELEN Puttock cursed under her breath. She couldn't find her favourite crimson lipstick. Her right hand danced across the dressing table, searching frantically for her make-up bag. She cursed again as she scattered jewellery on to the carpet and knocked over her perfume bottle. A sweet, sickly scent filled the air as her eyes flicked towards the bedside alarm clock. It was two minutes to seven.

Jeannie would be here soon, and Helen was nowhere near ready. She hated rushing her make-up. If she was going to the dancin' she wanted to look her best. She'd spent too long playing with her little boys David and Michael and chatting to husband George. It was great to have him home on leave. It wasn't often they were together as a family. Yes, it had been good since he'd arrived back from Germany. They'd been going through a sticky patch recently. They'd had their rows, but maybe things would get better. She hoped so anyway.

It was a short journey to Helen's house in Earl Street in the Scotstoun area of Glasgow for big sister Jeannie. She lived in Kelso Street just down the road in Yoker. Jeannie had moved into her council house with her three boys after separating from her husband. Jeannie loved a night on the town. There was nothing better than a few whiskies and then off to the jiggin'. There was an extra skip in her step as she dodged the puddles on the way to Helen's house.

Helen and Jeannie were very close. As kids they had rarely fought and, as teenagers, they had a great deal in common. They shared make-up and talked endlessly about boyfriends and their hopes for the future. They often laughed and joked about the time they worked as "clippies", taking the fares in their uniforms on the buses after leaving school.

They'd survived a troubled home life. Helen was 18 when her mum Jean split from their dad. Jean Gowans was a strong woman and she was left to take care of Helen, Jeannie, brother Sam and younger sister Patsy. Times were hard, money was tight and family life was often strained. Helen was a popular girl, never short of a date during her teenage years. She loved a laugh and a joke and a night out with the girls. She was also beginning to enjoy the company of men. She discovered she was good at flirting, and secretly relished the feeling of warmth she got from that intimacy.

Helen was staying with her brother Sam in Wokingham, Surrey, when she first set eyes on George. He was a soldier who loved Army life and had signed on for 11 years. Helen was smitten. There was an immediate chemistry between them. She fell for George's rugged good looks. The dashing soldier felt the same way, and when Helen returned to Glasgow, they arranged to be married.

Life as a soldier's wife was not easy with George often away for weeks on end. She spent her days working and her nights alone in their new house. Despite her outgoing personality, Helen found it hard to cope with her sudden change in lifestyle.

When George was away, she yearned for him to come home. When he returned the niggly arguments would start, for no apparent reason. Then, out of the blue, George was sent with his unit on a long-term posting to the British Army of the Rhine in Bad Godesburg in West Germany. She couldn't bear the thought of being apart for months. She packed her bags and followed him.

It was the worst thing Helen could have done. Life in Germany turned an ordinary, outgoing larger-than-life girl into a virtual recluse. She was a married woman with two children. She couldn't speak the language and she was unable to break into the Army wife clique. She was an outsider in a strange country and she hated every minute of it. George, a corporal, was away on duty during most of the day, so she found herself with time on her hands. She became depressed and desperately missed her old life in Glasgow. She had no friends, and the brief moments of love and support she snatched when George was off-duty did little to compensate for the long hours of misery. She put up with life in Germany for a year. Then one day she announced to her soldier husband: "I'm going home to Glasgow to stay with my mum." Being back with mum was a godsend for Helen. She had an immediate companion and someone to help out with the children. Anyway it would be handy for school when David was old enough, she thought.

Most importantly of all she was back with her girlfriends. Her first few weeks in Glasgow were a social whirl. She had a lot of catching up to do. Suddenly her days were filled with girlie chat and cups of tea with the other young mums in the area. She was 29, but it was just like being a teenager again.

Helen had always loved dancing and her friends talked excitedly about Palais Night for the over-25s at the Barrowland. Suddenly George and Germany seemed a lifetime away. Helen started to enjoy life again. Maybe the days were a slog with two young children, but she always had the nights out to look forward to. And her mum was always willing to baby-sit. When she could afford it she either went out with Jeannie or some of the other local girls.

George knew that Helen was going out at nights, but what else could he expect? She was a young woman, and after all he enjoyed nights with the boys when he was off duty, so she was entitled to some pleasure. Anyway her letters suggested she was happy and contented and loving being back "home." George came home to Glasgow whenever he could. He really missed the kids. When he did return he quickly settled back into domestic life. He didn't mind looking after the children. His short few days with them in Glasgow were so precious. It wasn't a surprise to George when Helen announced on Thursday, October 30, 1969 - the night before Hallowe'en - that she was going out with Jeannie. They planned to go to the Barrowland. He didn't want her to go dancing. To a traditional man brought up in a working-class town it wasn't right for a young mum to go out without her husband. But fun-loving Helen insisted, and he eventually gave in - as he always did. George would be baby-sitter for the night. He was quite happy. He would get the wee ones off to bed and put his feet up. Helen would be late back. He decided he would give them the 10 shillings for a taxi home and he knew Helen had a key. As he settled down to play with David and Michael he heard a knock at the front door.

Helen was still trying to fix her hair as Jeannie burst into the bedroom. The first thing Helen noticed was that her sister was looking particularly attractive that night. The burden, stress and weight of her recent separation seemed to have lifted from her slender shoulders. There were fewer worry lines around her eyes. It was great to see her looking so well, Helen thought to herself, as she dragged the brush through her brown hair for a final time.

Helen was looking good too. She didn't have a lot to choose from in her wardrobe, but she'd decided on a black short-sleeved dress with gold buttons, brown tights, green nylon knickers, a blue and black underslip and black strap shoes. She pulled on her fake ocelot fur coat. It was the height of fashion and Helen was proud of that coat. The other girls liked it too. It made her feel special. With a final glance in the mirror she was finally ready to go.

The two sisters had read about the murder of Mima McDonald two months earlier. They also knew about the killing of Pat Docker in 1968. Like them, both women had excitedly done their make-up and looked forward to a night of dance and escape at the Barrowland. There was talk of a sadistic killer who stalked the famous dance hall looking for women on a night out - just like them. But things had calmed down since the McDonald murder. Fewer people were going to the dancing because of the publicity about the killing. But it was two months ago and the police hadn't been able to prove anything. Anyway, they would be all right. Safety in numbers. They were meeting up with their friends,

Marion and Jean. They would be part of a crowd. Nobody would be out looking to harm them. They would be safe. Anyway, you can't sit in the house every night worrying about what MIGHT happen. Life just would not be worth living if they did that. And they were young with a lot of life still ahead.

It was around 8pm when Helen and Jeannie came teetering down the stairs. They said good-bye to George before stepping out into the chilly October night. Kids were out guisin' that night, the traditional Hallowe'en activity when they would learn a song, poem and daft wee joke to recite to neighbours or folk in the street in the hope of getting a few pennies, fruit or a bag of sweets. They pestered the dance hall-bound couples with the well-practised plea "gonnae gies ma Hallowe'en". But the sisters didn't have time to stop. There was a night's dancing waiting and fun to be had. They had a bus to catch.

The Glasgow of 27 years ago was a vastly different place to what it is today. Many old, blackened slums remained and the massive city centre clean-up had still to take place. A pound of best steak cost eight shillings (40p) - good mince a mere five shillings (25p) a pound. A night on the town was just as cheap. DJ Tony Blackburn was presenting the breakfast show on Radio One, Scotland crashed out of the World Cup after being beaten 3-2 by West Germany in a bruising qualifier, and Sheena Drummond was preparing to become the first Scots beauty to compete in Miss World. Paddy Meehan was jailed for life - later to be pardoned - for the killing of 72-year-old Rachel Ross. A new Ford Zodiac cost around £1500 and trouble was erupting on the streets of Belfast. But in Glasgow the chat in the pubs was always about Rangers and Celtic. Men supped their pints and speculated about the Parkhead side possibly selling Tommy Gemmell. Rangers had just dropped Jim Baxter for the game against Dunfermline. The miners were threatening to strike.

Thursday nights were the best winchin' nights at the Barrowland in the 1960s. Pay packets were ripped open and married men made their excuses to their wives and stepped out for "a couple of pints with the boys". But they would really be Barrowland-bound. They soaped off their tell-tale wedding rings, drowned themselves in cheap aftershave and got ready for action. They were out for a few drinks, a spot of jiggin' and who knows, maybe even a "lumber". Stolen kisses and cuddles in the darkened corners of the ballroom, then back to her place before staggering home in the early hours of the morning. If you were really brave, you might just stay the whole night at her place. But there was always the niggling worry of having to explain it all to the wife in the morning. And was it really worth the hassle you'd get for the rest of the week? Glasgow's hard men also loved the Barrowland. They brought their own brand of "chib-rule" to the dance hall. They were always spoiling for a fight, and Thursday night battles were commonplace. Thursday nights were also exclusively for the over-25s. The sign above the famous ballroom screamed "Palais Night, 8pm - Midnight". Once the Barrowland doors closed behind you, it was time to shut out your worries and dance. You could lose yourself in there and with the sound of the band resounding through your head, you could become someone else for the night. It was worth waiting a whole week for the next Thursday.

Helen and Jeannie jumped on the bus in Dumbarton Road. Helen was determined to make it a great night, despite the fact she was having her period. They bought their tickets for the short trip to Glasgow Cross. They seemed to have so much to talk about and hardly noticed the Clyde shipyards and the blackened tenements which lined the route. The bus trip was great for planning the night. Who's getting the first round? Will we have a kitty instead? Do you think that guy with the dark eyes, light suit and nifty footwork who was there a fortnight ago will be out tonight? You do remember the man I'm talking about! The journey just flashed by, transporting the girls on to the next stage of their night out.

The bus drew into Glasgow Cross around 9pm. It was far too early to go to the dancing. It didn't really warm up until after ten, so they decided to go for a drink. Most of their companions at the Cross were heading for the pub. The sisters decided on the Trader's Tavern in Kent Street. It was the last hour before 10pm closing, so there was the usual clamour at the bar, but Helen and Jeannie managed to down three whiskies each. They had been joined by their friends Marion Cadder and Jean O'Donnell, but a steady stream of people were by that time heading across to the Barrowland, so they decided to follow.

There was a queue outside the dance hall. The girls walked the short distance from the pub and hurried along to join it. It wasn't unusual having to wait to get into the Barrowland. Thursday nights were always very popular. They eventually paid their four shillings (20p) and they were in.

The familiar stench of alcohol and stale cigarette reek filled their nostrils as Helen took off her prized coat. The place was jumping. They decided to try Geordie's Byre first. It was the smaller of the Barrowland's two halls where records boomed out at an eardrum-shattering level. Upstairs was the main dance floor where there was usually a live band on stage. They stayed downstairs for about half an hour before moving to the bigger hall. The floor was filled with couples throwing each other about. Every darkened corner of the dance hall seemed to be occupied by kissing and fumbling couples, their slowly-moving bodies picked out every few seconds by the light bouncing off the mirrored ball high up on the ceiling.

The music was thumping as a man asked Jeannie up to dance. She quite fancied him she thought as she made her way on to the floor. He said his name was John and he was a builder from Castlemilk. Everyone in Glasgow around that time was called John or Jim - especially if they were married. But the conversation with John was strained and difficult, partly because of the loud music but mostly because he seemed shy. Flushed with embarrassment, he even asked her "Do you come here often?" Jeannie immediately thought: "He's married." But despite his naive chat-up lines, Jeannie liked this man called John. He asked her to stay up for the next dance. They stayed on the floor together for the rest of the night.

Although Jeannie was pre-occupied by her new dancing partner, she couldn't help wondering what Helen was up to. She'd left her alone more dances ago than she cared to remember. Then she noticed a man leaning, almost nonchalantly, against a pillar. He was about 5ft 10in tall, aged around 30 and smartly dressed in a continental-style single-breasted suit. Unusually, he was wearing leather half boots, which weren't particularly fashionable. He seemed to be running his eye over the women. Jeannie thought she'd seen him before, possibly at the Barrowland, but it could have been the Plaza, she wasn't sure. She was struck by his elegance. He was so unlike most of the men who frequented the Barrowland. This man had a bit of style. Jeannie couldn't put her finger on exactly why her attention was drawn to this red-haired man, but she couldn't help staring at him.

SHE DIDN'T KNOW IT, BUT SHE HAD JUST LOOKED INTO THE EVIL EYES OF THE MURDERER BIBLE JOHN.

John moved quickly. He'd noticed the pretty brunette sitting on her own. He ran his eyes over her a couple of times and decided to "move in'. "Do you fancy a dance?" he said in what was for Glasgow a very posh accent. The girl stood up, transfixed by his smile and his eyes. There was something about his eyes which made her take his hand and follow him, as if in slow motion, on to the dance floor.

"Meet John," shrilled Helen as she swished past Jeannie, her black dress billowing. Jeannie looked round and saw her sister in the arms of the man who'd been standing at the pillar. Momentarily stunned, she blurted out: "No, YOU meet John," and she motioned towards her dancing partner. The foursome stopped dancing for a few seconds and had a good chuckle as the two Johns were introduced. "Everyone seems to be called John around here," joked Helen. The two couples finished their dance and sat down together.

Jeannie couldn't help noticing how well-mannered her sister's new friend was. He said and did all the right things, and he was so confident. He was so unlike most of the other men who were quick with the risqué joke or the smutty innuendo. There was something about this man, though, that Jeannie didn't like. But Helen seemed happy. She and John were never off the dance floor. She was having a ball and Jeannie was pleased. The night was turning into a real success.

BUT HELEN'S JOHN WAS TO SHOW HE HAD A DARKER SIDE - EVEN BEFORE HE LEFT THE BARROWLAND.

The band almost raised the nicotine-stained roof as they finished their set. They had been brilliant. Everyone cheered as they struck the last chord and the lights went up. Helen, Jeannie and the two Johns headed, exhausted, for the exit. They had been up for the last three numbers and Helen's dress was beginning to stick to her as the tiny beads of sweat trickled down her back. The two Johns went to the gents, Helen's John emerged holding his scarf which he smoothed down in front of him before putting on his coat. He did it in such a strange way. What a mother's boy, mused Jeannie. As they made their way towards the cloakroom, Jeannie decided she wanted cigarettes. She'd passed her pack around a couple of times during the evening and now she suddenly realised she had none left. She popped her money into the slot and pushed the button for her favourite Embassy filters. Nothing happened. "My money's stuck," she shouted to her sister. Helen and the two Johns walked over to see if they could help. In a matter of seconds, Helen's John turned from a well-mannered, well-spoken man into an angry, short-tempered firebrand. It was as if somebody had flicked a switch inside his head.

John barked: "Where's the manager? I want to see the manager." He started waving his arms about, ignoring the stares of the homeward-bound couples. Helen and Jeannie tried to defuse the situation. It was all becoming a bit embarrassing. They told him the money didn't matter. They would get cigarettes elsewhere. He'd never track down the manager at this time of night anyway. But Helen's John was in full flight now and, with one sneering glance, shot down the girls' protests.

The manager arrived on the scene. He was the kind of man you did not argue with. Stocky-built, he had a long scar on one side of his face. His bulbous nose seemed to go off in different directions - undoubtedly a souvenir of a "disagreement" with a punter. John ignored the manager's "lived-in" look and carried on regardless. He demanded that Jeannie get her money back. He was pointing and gesticulating. He was like some kind of deranged dictator. He demanded his own way - or else. The sisters were astonished by the change in the man who had been a delight to be with only moments earlier. He argued with dogged determination. Always lucid, but never swearing. He sounded well-educated. He knew exactly how to make his point.

The manager was having none of John's rantings. The argument became more and more heated as the ballroom boss refused to back down and brushed him off by telling him to see the assistant manager downstairs. John was raging. He stormed off to get the money back, but on the way turned and said chillingly and deliberately in his posh voice: "My father said these places are dens of iniquity. They set fire to this place to get the insurance money and did it up with the money they got." Jeannie didn't know what iniquity meant. It wasn't a word she used. She thought she'd heard it once before at Chapel, but wasn't sure. She noticed John whispering into Helen's ear. Helen was shaking her head, as if in disbelief. Then he took out what looked like an ID card. A knowing smile played on Helen's lips as she read the card. Jeannie moved over to try and read the card, but quick-as-a-flash John stuffed it back into his pocket. "Why can't I get to see it,?' asked Jeannie.

"You know what happens to nosey folk," sneered John, tapping the side of his nose.

Helen, Jeannie and the two Johns stepped out into the mayhem that is Glasgow's closing time. They headed for the taxi rank at Glasgow Cross, a few hundred yards away. Jeannie and her John led the way, Helen and the other John a few paces behind. It only took minutes. There was a queue at the rank, and Jeannie's John announced that he was going off for the late bus at George Square. Jeannie shouted that she hoped to see him again as he headed off into the distance.

SHE WOULD NEVER AGAIN SET EYES ON CASTLEMILK JOHN.

Helen's John was getting anxious. He'd got rid of the other John, but Jeannie was a problem. How could he get Helen on her own? Would Helen go off alone with him? He'd already persuaded her to allow him to see her home - that was something. But the two girls lived near each other. He had to think of something, some plan to separate the two of them.

ALREADY JOHN HAD MURDER ON HIS MIND.

Soon it was their turn at the head of the taxi queue, and the three of them piled in. The conversation was strained. John seemed uneasy about Jeannie being there. But Jeannie was NOT happy about John. There was SOMETHING about this man she didn't like, and the incident at the cigarette machine only served to fuel her suspicions.

The taxi left Glasgow Cross on the 20-minute journey along Argyle Street, up Dumbarton Road and into Scotstoun. The late shift was just finishing at the city's docks. The cab sped past an advertising hoarding which screamed: "After work you need a Guinness." The threesome didn't notice the tiny newsagent's shop which was still displaying that night's billboards. The headline of the day was "Glasgow sex Maniac Sent to Carstairs."

John didn't try and hide his disapproval that Jeannie was in the taxi. At first he was solemn and withdrawn, then he started talking, slowly at first, then more enthusiastically.

ALTHOUGH THE SISTERS DIDN'T KNOW IT, THEY WERE ABOUT TO HEAR THE WORDS WHICH WOULD BRAND THIS KILLER BIBLE JOHN.

He started off talking about golf and said he had a cousin who once had a hole in one. Then he dramatically switched tack, and despite the company he was in, he pronounced his disapproval of married women going to the Barrowland. He then talked generally of "adulterous women". He said something about his sister, then immediately tried to retract it. There was a remark about football and the bitter rivalry between Rangers and Celtic. When he was asked what he did at Hogmanay, he said he didn't drink, but prayed.

Religion was the topic for the rest of the taxi ride. John said he was an agnostic but did know parts of the Bible. He then said something about foster homes or foster children, Moses and a woman being stoned or standing at a well. It was strange to hear these Old Testament references, thought Jeannie. She remembered parts from her childhood when she attended Chapel regularly.

The exact Bible reference uttered that night has never been established, but detectives believe it was a reference to Moses and the bulrushes from  Exodus Ch 2 v. 3/4:..

*"And when she could no longer hide him, she took for him an ark of bulrushes, and daubed it with slime and with pitch, and put the child therein; and she laid it in the flags by the river's bank; and his sister stood afar off, to wait what would be done to him."*

By this time Jeannie was scared. Then another conversation in the taxi made her hate this strange Bible-quoting man. She'd run out of cigarettes inside the ballroom and had lost her money in the machine. She had been desperate for a puff for the last hour, but thought John didn't smoke. He'd never produced any cigarettes during the evening. But suddenly he produced a pack of her favourite Embassy. He offered them to Helen, but didn't take one himself. He then started to put them away. Angry, Jeannie asked him for a cigarette but he ignored her. His arm was still full out holding the packet, so out of sheer spite she took three cigarettes and stuffed them into her jacket. She would show him. She'd teach him not to be so rude. There was no need for that type of behaviour, she thought.

As the taxi drew into Earl Street, Bible John insisted that the cab go the 10 minutes further up the road to Jeannie's house in Yoker, before returning to Helen's house in Scotstoun. Jeannie was anxious about this move. She hadn't liked the way the conversation had gone in the taxi. If it wasn't obvious before, it was now. John wanted her out of the way so he could be alone with her sister. But Helen was a big girl. She was 29 after all. She knew her sister would be excited about this handsome man who was taking her home from the dancing. She'd be looking forward to a fly kiss and a cuddle. What George didn't know wouldn't hurt him. After all it was only a kiss and a cuddle.

But somehow Jeannie wasn't keen on letting John know where her house was, so when the taxi approached the roundabout at the bottom of her street she told the driver to stop and jumped out. She waved good-bye to Helen. John just sat there stony-faced. He didn't even acknowledge her cheerios.

IT WAS THE LAST TIME SHE SAW HER SISTER ALIVE.

The taxi driver doubled back and dropped Helen and Bible John in Earl Street. The pair walked towards a close mouth at number 95, 100 yards from where she lived at number 129. The time was 12.30am.

But it wasn't the last time Bible John was seen that night. Around 2am on the Friday morning a near-empty night service bus travelling along Dumbarton Road picked him up near the junction with Gardner Street. He looked a pale imitation of the dapper man who had wooed Helen earlier that evening at the Barrowland. His clothes were a mess. His shirt was hanging out. His Italian suit jacket was filthy. He looked as if he had been rolling in the mud. He had a red weal on his cheek. A passenger who was sitting near him tutted. "He's been fighting," thought the man. "When will these people ever learn?" But he hadn't been fighting.

BIBLE JOHN CARRIED THE MARKS OF A MURDERER.

He didn't have far to go to find a safe haven. He jumped off the bus at the Gray Street stop outside the Lorne Hotel in Sauchiehall Street. Detectives believe he had friends who lived just a few minutes away. He knew he could get a bed there for the night. He was tired. His friends were both in their 70s and wouldn't be up to see him arrive. But he knew they'd be pleased to see him in the morning.

Archie MacIntyre always took his faithful black Labrador, Smokey, out for an early morning walk. Come rain, hail or shine, the 40-year-old roadman was always to be seen around the Earl Street area. He usually timed his walk to start around 7am, which gave him time for a quick stroll, back for a bite of breakfast and off to work. This morning was no different to any other. Archie followed Smokey down the stair at 95 Earl Street.

Usually Smokey would run off ahead, but his master noticed him sniffing round the back court. Archie walked over."Come on boy," he shouted, trying to attract Smokey's attention, "get away from these old rags." Then Smokey started whimpering. Archie took a closer look. He immediately felt sick, his whole mind enveloped by a numbing sensation.

Helen Puttock's body, draped in her beloved fur coat, was lying in a crumpled heap. She was a strange colour. Life had drained from her features. Archie sprinted back into the close, his heart pounding. Breathless, he tried knocking on a couple of doors. No reply. He needed to get to a phone. He remembered the box across the street, grabbed the receiver and dialled 999. The dial appeared to move in slow motion as he anxiously waited to be connected. "Let me speak to the police," he blurted. When Archie plucked up enough courage to return to the back court, the police and ambulance men were already there.

Helen Puttock had gone with Bible John to the back court. There was nothing wrong with a "wee winch" she thought. But something had gone horribly wrong as they walked together hand in hand into the darkened alleyway.

Something made Helen Puttock run that night. But she wasn't getting away. Like a wild beast with its prey in sight, Bible John chased after her. She could hear the sound of his panting getting nearer and nearer. She made for the railway embankment, but it was hopeless. Bible John grabbed her coat. He punched her in the head until she slumped into unconsciousness. He pulled Helen back into the close at number 95. Her heels dragged along the grass, leaving a tram-like impression. Bible John took off her tights, wrapping the garment tightly round her neck. Then he squeezed the very life out of poor Helen Puttock.

At some point during the frenzied attack, Helen was brutally raped. Nobody had heard a thing in that quiet, dank back court. What should have been a fun-filled night out with her sister ended in Helen Puttock's horrific murder.

George Puttock was getting worried about his wife. She hadn't come home last night. That wasn't particularly unusual. She often stayed with friends. But he was curious about the police activity in the nearby back court. As he stepped outside he was met by Superintendent Joe Beattie. "My wife's not come home," he told the grim-faced detective. Superintendent Beattie walked to the back court where Helen's body lay. George could only stare and shake his head as he got closer. Helen's familiar fur coat was lying in the mud.

But there was something else about Helen's limp body which caught Joe Beattie's attention. There was something poking out from under her armpit - something white. The detective lifted her arm, and out fell Helen's blood-stained sanitary towel. It had been carefully placed there by her killer.

Bible John had satisfied his lust for blood. As the mother-of two lay dead in the mud and dirt yards from the warmth and love of her husband and wee boys, her sadistic murderer disappeared into the night. The cool killer had stalked, coveted and captured his prey. But he'd made one fatal error. In his frenzied sex attack he left a semen stain on Helen Puttock's clothing And there was something else. There was a deep bite mark on her tortured body.

# CHAPTER FIVE

## JOHN McINNES - A DISCIPLE OF DEATH?

*"For as often as ye eat this bread, and drink this cup, ye do shew the Lord's death till he come."*
1 Corinthians 11:26

JOHN Irvine McInnes fancied a drink. He glanced at the clock. It would soon be opening time. Dragging himself out of bed, he smiled wistfully as he remembered last night. He'd been at the Barrowland. Thursday nights were always great fun. He'd gone on his own, but that was all right because there was always plenty of "talent" about. But he really needed that drink now. His throat was dry and his voice husky. It must have been the dust from that dance hall floor. It was his day off and he had it all planned. He fancied a game of dominoes with some of the pensioners down at the pub. He thought some of them were repulsive and smelled of stale beer, but it was good fun trying to cheat them out of their pension money. Some of them didn't even know what time of day it was after a few jars. The sun shone through a chink in his bedroom curtains, its beam landing on his smart Italian suit which he'd casually thrown over the bedroom chair when he'd got in from the dancing.

As he pulled on his clothes, McInnes remembered the

pretty girl he'd been dancing with. She was a real looker. She'd even allowed him to walk her home. He turned on the radio. The news bulletin was just starting as it crackled into life. He stopped what he was doing and listened. He smiled...

McInnes spent a great deal of his social life at The Old Ship Inn in Stonehouse. He went there to meet his brother Hector, chatting about work, family and life generally over his favourite tipple - a half of whisky and a half-pint of beer.

If Hector was not around then McInnes chatted to the regular faces, wrinkled men from the village who had known life. Most were former miners whose free time now centred around the village pub. There was no shortage of places to drink in Stonehouse. Maybe it had a lack of shops providing the basics of life, but there was never a shortage of drinking dens.

John McInnes loved The Old Ship Inn. It was a short walk from his mother's house, a brisk two minutes if he didn't bump into some village worthy on the way. Many afternoons he'd leave his mother's neat, cream-painted house at 26 Queen Street - one of the shortest streets in the village and known locally as "The Back Road". As he stepped from the garden path onto the pavement he glanced lovingly at his prized, gleaming green Ford Cortina which he kept parked outside.

Many thought it strange that McInnes actually walked past another pub, just yards from the house, on his way to The Old Ship. The distinctive black-and-white painted Cross Keys Inn, is a typically couthy, village pub with a welcoming atmosphere. But McInnes opted not to drink there often. It was too near home. Too near the watchful eye of his elderly mum Elizabeth. The family were members of the strict Brethren sect. Because of her beliefs, she frowned on those who drank alcohol, and she didn't want her son doing it. She also frowned on gambling. In fact, she frowned on most of the things that her son wanted to do. Life was easier if he did his drinking out of sight, around the corner and 50 yards or so along the street at The Old Ship. She couldn't see him in there. He was happy in there.

The Old Ship Inn on New Street now stands empty, metal grilles covering the window spaces. When the last pint had been pulled in the early 1990s, it closed its door on a chapter of the Bible John saga.

McInnes' mother dominated him. Villagers believed that Elizabeth McInnes' influence extended to insisting that he use her maiden name of Irvine as his first name. It had a ring to it, she thought. Certainly a bit more out of the ordinary than the name John he was first given. In later years he reverted to his original name - especially when out socially. It was a way of rebelling against his mother and the religion he despised.

McInnes liked to look smart when he went out. His mum liked him looking good too. Although he was an adult, had been married and had spent many years away from the family home, he still listened to, and obeyed, his mother. And if she thought he was looking good then he could relax. None of the other pub regulars put on the same style as McInnes. He liked his expensive, well-cut suits, his freshly-laundered shirts, and often wore his distinctive blue and red striped Scots Guards regimental tie. He was often caught glancing at himself in the pub mirror, checking his appearance and preening his hair.

Despite his dapper look and apparent aloofness, McInnes liked to mingle and mix with the village's elder statesmen. They would be there when he arrived - always during the afternoon - sitting around the beer-splashed domino table. McInnes smiled as he strolled in to hear the familiar clatter of the nicotine-stained domino pieces. "Deal me in next game," would be his friendly shout as he ordered up his drink from Margaret, the barmaid.

McInnes enjoyed a flutter - some said he was a compulsive gambler. He would spend hours trying to win a pittance at the domino table. The stakes were low - pennies rather than pounds, no-one had much spare cash, but it was a thrill for McInnes to try taking money from these pensioners. He would never drink much during these games. He had to keep his wits about him. But he faced tough competition from his opponents. These were domino fanatics who played day in day out and had done so for many more years than McInnes. They took money from him every time. His half and half pint - a long-time popular combination for the working man - seemed to last for hours as he slowly sipped away at the glasses, trying hard to keep track of the game. He was a strange sight perched there, dressed to the nines. To these worthy pensioners McInnes was from a strange world and he rarely gave much away.

Two of the old men glanced at each other as McInnes spoke. They had heard him utter these phrases before. McInnes was quoting the Bible. He'd drop these lines into conversation as others chatted about the weather, their racing bets or the price of beer. The men couldn't claim to be religious but they knew enough to realise what McInnes was saying. This was one of his favourites - Corinthians, they remembered him telling them. He often recited chunks from the Bible to anyone who would listen. They always remembered the lines starting something like: "When I was a child . . ."

McInnes knew them exactly, word for word, fault-free . . .

" . . .When I was a child, I spake as a child, I understood as a child, I thought as a child: But when I became a man, I put away childish things.

"For now we see through a glass, darkly; but then face to face: now I know in part; but then shall I know even as also I am known.

"And now abideth faith, hope, charity, these three; but the greatest of these is charity."

Corinthians 13:1-13

They just ignored him. He stopped soon enough when he realised no-one was paying that much attention. The old men knew religion was one subject to steer well clear of. Because the man they were playing dominoes with was now known as Bible John. He made no secret of it. Ever since he had proudly announced in the pub one day that he had been a suspect in the Barrowland murder inquiry he'd been known locally as Bible John. He thought it was amusing. He liked being the centre of attention, the main man. He told his pub pals he had been picked up by the police and taken in for FOUR identity parades. He was proud of the fact he was a suspect. He certainly looked like the man whose picture was in the newspapers, so it was understandable the police wanted to talk to him. He liked the Bible, and the real Bible John had supposedly quoted the good book to one of his victims. So he could understand why villagers thought he was a suspect. He couldn't argue with that. But he'd never been picked out at one of these line-ups. He'd been ruled out as a suspect. But he enjoyed the notoriety the nickname gave him. He boasted shamelessly about the ID parades. He thought it was great - just so long as mother didn't find out.

Villager George Golder remembered: "He played dominoes with my father. He liked the company of that

55

older set in the pub. But my dad and his pals used to joke about how easy it was taking money off him. He didn't have a clue. In fact the old men waited for him coming in so they could win some money. He was often in my dad's house and he would usually arrive with a half or quarter bottle of whisky. I remember he had an unusual way of walking. He took big long strides and moved with a skipping movement as if walking on the balls of his feet.

"I met him after he came back from one identity parade. We were standing in the street and he told me all about it. I'll never forget it.

"ALL HE COULD DO WAS LAUGH AND LAUGH."

As well as the dominoes, McInnes loved a punt on the horses. His mother certainly wouldn't have approved. He strolled from her house to the bookmaker's in the village's Argyle Street. It was owned by Larkhall-based bookie William Weir. McInnes placed his bets with William Clarkson who ran the Stonehouse shop. He remembers him as a regular, if not compulsive, gambler. "He was always well spoken. He'd only put a couple of pounds on the horses. He liked his gambling," recalled Mr Clarkson.

"I wasn't surprised when the police announced he was a suspect. He was known by the nickname Bible John for years. I remember once he came in. He'd been away for some time and said he'd been in England and been picked up by the police and put into an identification parade for the murders.

"He told people he had been questioned. The photofit looked so like him."

Another meeting sticks in Mr Clarkson's mind. It was on a bus going from Stonehouse to Glasgow. Mr Clarkson was heading towards Larkhall to see his boss and hand over the takings from the day before.

"McInnes looked dreadful. I can't remember exactly what day of the week it was. It sticks in my mind that it was a day near the weekend. I asked him if he was late for work. He turned towards me, and putting his head in his hands, said: 'I had a helluva night last night.' I've no idea what he had been up to but now it makes me wonder..."

It was yet another incident - around the time of McInnes' involvement in the Bible John probe - that left a lasting impact on another local. It was a moment which will haunt the woman for the rest of her life - the moment she looked straight into the piercing eyes of Bible John. Even today, 27 years later, she can't erase the memory. She finds it hard to talk about it. She knew John McInnes well. He knew her family and it was not unusual for him to call at her home in Stonehouse. But this time it was very different.

Jane Reid - we have changed her name to protect her identity - opened the door that day. She was taken aback. It was McInnes. He walked in past her, heading for the front room. She immediately felt a chill. There was something different about the man she knew so well, something frightening about his presence.

She followed him into the room and before she could say anything she caught his eye. He started to speak. But it was all too much for Jane. The look on his face, the sound and tone of his voice - it was haunting. She remembered the stories about him being quizzed by the police and taken to the line-ups in Glasgow. Suddenly she felt threatened. She felt uncomfortable in her own home. She had to escape, get away from him. She didn't want him near her.

Jane ran from the room, out into the hallway and pulled open the front door. She was agitated, breathless and afraid. The fresh air hit her like a stone wall. She was outside, away from McInnes who hadn't even moved. He stayed inside her home. Jane was in a panic. She didn't know what to do. She looked around. Then she remembered. A neighbour had gone out earlier that day. He would be back but exactly when she didn't know. She had no choice. She had to wait for someone to come to her assistance. There was no way she wanted to go back inside the house alone. She waited outside her own home for two hours.

They seemed like the longest two hours of her life. The neighbour's arrival was such a relief. Jane almost broke down. Babbling, she blurted out what had happened and her concerns. The neighbour - at first puzzled - listened intently.

"I just want him out of the house. Please get him out now!" Jane screamed.

Seconds later, Bible John had been given his marching orders in no uncertain terms. Despite the known police interest in McInnes, Jane never reported the incident. She remains reluctant to discuss the events at length. A friend who she confided in revealed: "She was petrified. She said she felt threatened, intimidated by McInnes' look and how he was speaking to her. There are only two or three people in Stonehouse who were told about this. She has her own reasons for not discussing it but ever since that day she was convinced that he was the real Bible John, the man who killed."

McInnes was born in Stonehouse at 6am on Saturday, September 10, 1938. It was a home birth. At the time his mother Elizabeth and father Robert Samson McInnes were living at an address known as 9 Holding in Sidehead Road. The house was set among a cluster of small farm properties overlooking the rolling hills of

Lanarkshire. Robert and Elizabeth had married in Stonehouse on Thursday, April 21, 1921. Nineteen days after McInnes was born, proud father Robert, a house furnisher and draper, officially registered the birth with village assistant registrar, Peter Adair.

McInnes spent an uneventful childhood in Stonehouse. The one difference setting McInnes' upbringing apart from that of the other local children was his parents' religious leanings. He went to the village primary school and, in later years, was pushed along with his brother Hector and sister Etta into taking entry exams for Hamilton Academy. His parents were comfortably off - not wealthy. They ran a shop in the village, a drapery. Years later they set McInnes up in business in a sweet shop in Stonehouse's King Street but it didn't work out.

McInnes did his National Service with the Scots Guards. He joined 45 Platoon in Pirbright, Surrey, in the summer of 1957, three years after the death of his father from natural causes. But his lack of confidence failed to impress Army chiefs and, after his basic training, he was "back-squadded" to 46 Platoon's "L" company. He was taken under the wing of platoon instructor Lance Corporal Gus Macdonald.

He recalled McInnes' time in the forces, telling newspapers: "He was an awkward boy with no confidence. He seemed very upset by the death of his father and always struck me as a sad figure."

In his spare time Gus even helped McInnes by taking him over the Army assault course to help him pass his training second time round.

"I tried to knock him into shape and give him some self-confidence. He never gave much away about himself but I knew that his father's death had a big impact on him.

"He wasn't a drinker and we never socialised when we were off shift," Gus added.

When McInnes finally passed out in 1958 he gave Gus a silver cigarette case, engraved with a map of Britain, as a token of his gratitude.

"You could never have disliked him. He just seemed to be so shy and he kept himself to himself . . ."

Two years later Gus and his wife bumped into McInnes while he was working in McGregor's furniture store in Sauchiehall Street, Glasgow.

"I was amazed to see him. He was immaculately dressed. He was wearing the regimental tie. He was so full of confidence. The shy boy I knew had disappeared and he looked as if he was making a right go of it. I was really pleased to see the changes in him.

"We liked a £180 suite and he came back a few minutes later and said we could have it for £150. When my wife thanked him he said that one good turn deserved another.

"You could never have said he was a bad boy when I knew him - he was just sad and away from home."

While Gus recalls McInnes as a non-drinker and a likeable character, William Sloan who slept in the next bed in the Army barracks tells a different story.

"I suppose I knew him best. He was a cold fish. He could be cunning and a bit of a user. He went out drinking one night instead of cleaning his kit. We all pitched in and did it for him so he wouldn't be in trouble. But instead of being grateful he just went out again the next night and did the same thing.

"I didn't like him much - but I would never have figured him for a murderer," said William.

Another Army pal was retired draper James

O'Donnell. He twice worked with the man he knew as Irvine McInnes.

"I couldn't believe my eyes when I read about the link between McInnes and Bible John.

"I first came across him when we both worked in Rowans, the clothing shop in Buchanan Street, Glasgow. He was well turned out - immaculate in fact - and a very quiet young man."

The pair were reunited when James joined 45 Platoon in Pirbright, at the same time John McInnes was reporting for weaponry training.

"He had joined up about four months before me but had been back-squadded because he wasn't really cut out for the Army. When I moved on from Pirbright he was back-squadded again. When I read about him in the papers and then saw the photograph of his gravestone it brought back all the memories of him," James said.

In a strange twist it later emerged that McInnes' Army records went missing from Wellington Barracks in London. Officials said they believed the documents charting his service years may have been handed over to detectives at the time of the original police probe and not returned. All that was left behind in his file was a card showing that he had been discharged in July, 1959.

If McInnes had been apprehensive about leaving Stonehouse - especially his family - for life in the Army, then the experiences during that brief spell of regimental life could hardly have bolstered his confidence. It was only after his return to civilian life that he coped better and developed more social skills, thriving in his role as a furniture salesman.

Twenty-one-year-old Helen Crockett McQueen Russell - known as Ella - was a pretty girl, a coal-miner's daughter. She was four years younger than John

McInnes and came from Muirkirk in Ayrshire. Love blossomed quickly and after a whirlwind romance, he proposed. The bride-to-be's parents, Adam and Elizabeth, only met McInnes about twice before the wedding plans were announced. They were married in Muirkirk Parish Church on March 16, 1964. It was a small Brethren ceremony attended only by the closest family members. At the time of the wedding McInnes was an assistant manager in a furniture store. The couple's first child Lorna was born nine months after the wedding on December 2, 1964.

The couple later ran Innesfield, a private home for the elderly in Ayr. Staff remember McInnes' habit of climbing into elderly patients' beds, apparently to comfort them in times of distress. It seemed a bizarre act, but he was in charge and no-one questioned it.

Ella's cousin Helen MacMillan told newspapers: "That made me shudder when I looked back. At the time I was just a young girl of 19 and thought nothing of it, because I suppose I genuinely believed there was nothing untoward going on. I clearly remember the old folk suddenly going very quiet when this happened, perhaps out of fear."

Mrs McMillan, who lived with the newlyweds at the home, claimed she was conned out of £1,000 by McInnes after she loaned him cash. She believed he gambled her money away. He then went to work for the Carrick Furniture firm in Ayr. It is believed that McInnes may have booked himself into the Ailsa Psychiatric Institution in Ayr at a time when he was thought to be running from charges of embezzlement from his employers. Mrs McMillan also recalled how he loved a bet.

"He was a real gambler, the sort of man who would

bet on two flies climbing up a wall. But I wouldn't have described him as a real womaniser - for a start he was pretty ugly and would not have had much success. He thought the world of Ella and when I lived with them I remember him coming home with big silver trays of food he had persuaded a hotel to give him. I also remember his eyes were often red and watery, probably through lots of drink."

McInnes was once caught for drink driving and Mrs McMillan and Ella went together to the police station to bail him out. At that time Ella was pregnant with a baby she lost at birth. In early 1968, soon after the couple split, their son Kenneth was born. It was around this time that the first of the murders in the Bible John saga - the killing of Pat Docker - was committed. McInnes and Ella were divorced at Ayr on February 25, 1972.

During the period of the three Bible John killings, McInnes switched jobs. He was then employed by a US stamp trading firm working as the sales manager. He drove his green Ford Cortina to work every day. In his new job McInnes baffled colleagues by regularly quoting from the Bible. But McInnes fell foul of his new employers. They held weekly sales meetings to discuss targets and selling techniques on Thursday nights. These meetings were important. The boss could keep a check on how McInnes and the rest of the sales team performed. But McInnes had somewhere more important to go - the Barrowland. He and his boss often rowed after it was discovered that he was skipping these meetings to go to the Over-25 nights at the dance hall.

These clashes with his boss weren't the only work problems McInnes encountered. He didn't mix well with the other members of staff and suddenly walked out of the job. Surprisingly for a man obsessed by money he never bothered to claim the expenses due for that week. Colleagues said that he had gone off to Australia, but in truth nobody was certain of his whereabouts. In his later years McInnes spent some time living in the Lanarkshire village of Newarthill. But he was still a regular visitor to Stonehouse to see his family - mum, brother Hector and sister Etta - and his old pub pals.

McInnes' formative years were strongly influenced by his parents, who were strict followers of the Brethren sect. The young McInnes was forced to attend weekly meetings, whether it was at the Gospel Tent which was temporarily erected in Stonehouse, or in the Brethren Hall - now the Salvation Army local headquarters - in Hill Road. Brethren communities thrived in Lanarkshire's close-knit villages. The most fanatical of believers have little contact with the outside world, shunning public places and condemning drinking and smoking. For McInnes' mother and father a place such as the Barrowland dance hall would be seen as a "den of iniquity" and a "seat of the Devil." That disdain was aggravated by the Barrowland's location in the heart of Glasgow - a city seen by villagers of the Brethren belief as being evil and wicked. Anyone caught frequenting such places faced discipline and even suspension from receiving Communion. McInnes stalked the ballroom looking for women out for the night without their husbands. He hated them for being there, and he hated the Barrowland for what he believed it was - a den of iniquity.

For McInnes, whose years of indoctrination had shaped his view of the outside world, women - and especially those who went out dancing - were a problem. He saw them very much as inferior - women should be forbidden to wear make-up and fashionable, revealing clothes. It was quite simple. To Brethren their purpose in life was to raise children. They didn't believe that women should leave their youngsters at home to head out in the pursuit of pleasure - especially to somewhere as "evil" as a dance hall.

The Brethren movement traces its history from a meeting evangelists held in September 1833 at Powerscourt House near Dublin. Later, the movement split into the "Open" and "Exclusive" Brethren. Critics of the Exclusive Brethren slammed them as marriage wreckers, home breakers and destroyers of lives.

One theory explored by writer Norman Adams suggested that the answers to the Bible John mystery lay within the close-knit Exclusive Brethren. Families belonging to the sect in Central Scotland had been seen by detectives, claimed Adams, who said he was aware that the murders caused comment and speculation among the Exclusive followers.

In his book "Goodbye, Beloved Brethren", published in 1972, Adams wrote: "In searching for a killer such as Bible John one must theoretically narrow the field down to the type of man likely to quote freely from the Bible. Police do not think he is over religious, but a man with a normal, intelligent working knowledge of the Bible. Even so he made some impression on Helen Puttock and her sister on the taxi journey with his biblical quotations. Bible John could well have been brought up by a family with a strict religious background and this makes one immediately think of a minority religious group rather than the established church.

"Can it be that his years of segregation from the world outside, his close-knit family, the harsh measures inflicted during his upbringing, has had some effect on this young man? Certainly there have been some incredible changes in the outlook of Brethren youngsters once they have broken away from their Exclusive life. I have witnessed many such changes in Brethren youth.

"One young man, cast out by his family after 18 years in the movement, found it extremely difficult to adjust to a world which seemed as alien to him as a man from the past. Luckily, he had at his side the sort of friends needed to guide him through the first months of his new-found freedom. But even so, he was introduced to a life he had never before tasted. He was taken to public houses, to the cinema, to dance halls, football matches and he watched television for the first time. Such a dramatic transition could have had disastrous results. But his watchers kept him firmly on the straight and narrow and he was able to adjust. There were times when he wished he could return to his family, but the thought of the Exclusive church was the spur he needed to go it alone.

"The Bible has been blamed for more than one horrible murder. In May 1971, *The Times* reported the tragic case of a New York woman who severed the head of her five-year-old daughter. When her husband came home he found her "babbling incoherently". She told him: "God made me do it." In the Book of Judith, part of the Apocrypha, Judith, a Jewish widow, cut off the head of Holofernes, an invading general.

"In June the same year *The Times* reported the harrowing case of a teenage West Indian boy who was sacrificed by his immigrant parents in a ritual killing at their home in Reading, Berkshire. Before 16-year-old Keith Goring was finally strangled, his foot was cut and his blood daubed in crosses on the foreheads of his three brothers as they lay stretched on the floor. During the ritual the boy was made to cough for long periods to free his sister from the Devil. The couple were members of the Pentecostal faith, a revival sect widely supported in the West Indies, and the boy was killed "during some sort of sacrifice during a session of fasting and meditation".

"The mental torture suffered by some unfortunate (Brethren) members has resulted in them taking some extreme escape routes, whilst others have found sanctuary in a sanatorium. Bible John may well be a more extreme manifestation."

Whatever went on inside the head of John Irvine McInnes one thing was abundantly clear. He was tormented to a degree that drove him to the brink. Was it the death of his father, the break-up of his marriage, the death of his child at birth, his rejection of the Brethren movement, the feeling that he had disappointed his mother - and continued doing so with his visits to the pubs and dance halls? Was it all these factors building up into a climax of emotional turmoil that left him helpless and ill-equipped to cope with his life? Or was it simply guilt - the burden of carrying the terrible truth that only he knew, that he was the real Bible John, the killer? He could put on a brave face for the outside world but behind closed doors this wretched man sank into the deepest, darkest recesses of depression that ate him up and forced him into dead ends. He could see no way out and there was no-one he could turn to for help, advice or even just the comfort of sharing his problems. Yes, he could have shared some of the emotional upset he was suffering but perhaps he was keeping the biggest secret of all - that he was a killer. Perhaps that was the hardest thing. Perhaps that was the brick wall he came up against time and time again. He tried drowning his torment and self-inflicted sorrows in drink. He put on a happy-go-lucky facade when he was in the pub, but often that mask slipped. The Bible passages would come out again as McInnes looked for an escape route. Instead he would simply catapult himself deeper into morbidity.

These black hours of despair drove him to extreme measures. Villagers spoke of him attempting suicide on three, possibly four occasions. One incident was well known in the village. When McInnes ran the sweet shop in Stonehouse he suddenly vanished. It was another shopkeeper, Willie Ramsay, the local fishmonger whose shop was next door, who eventually walked into McInnes' premises. McInnes had attempted to kill himself. Exactly how is lost in the mist of time but two theories are offered. One is that he had tried to hang himself, the other was that he had slashed his own throat. Whatever method he had chosen it was either a cry for help or he seriously believed there was no way forward and he wanted death to be his salvation and escape.

For John Irvine McInnes, that escape eventually came in April, 1980.

Margaret, the barmaid, was on duty in The Old Ship Inn on Tuesday, April 29. The pub was busy enough and she had been rushed off her feet pulling pints. There was the occasional outburst of laughter above the drone of chat. Most of the small band of regulars were there, and a game of dominoes was well underway. It was just a typical night. Margaret looked up as McInnes walked into the bar. She immediately noticed he didn't give his customary cheery smile, heralding his arrival. He walked to the bar and ordered up his usual - a half pint of beer and a whisky. Margaret noticed he was down in the mouth, a bit depressed, but that wasn't entirely unusual for a man who was prone to mood swings. He'd earned himself that sort of reputation in a community where men and women had enough on their minds trying to make ends meet without taking on others' worries. That night he didn't spend as long as he normally did in the pub, but he drank more than usual. Something was eating away at McInnes.

Sixteen years after that night Margaret remembers: "He was depressed. I'd seen him like that before. He was often down in the dumps. Everyone talked about it. He needed help but it just wasn't available in these days. But his mood didn't really change. He was really unhappy about something. That was the last time I saw him."

McInnes finished the last drops from his two glasses and set off on the short walk to his mother's home. He glanced occasionally at the street life, paying little attention to the other villagers spilling out of the pubs and heading home. Nothing registered in his mind. He was oblivious to everyone. He had made up his mind about what he was going to do. Nothing would sway him from that agenda. He walked into Queen Street, passing the Cross Keys, and up the short garden path to the front door. John Irvine McInnes didn't turn back for a final glance at the outside world. He needed to be inside the protective walls of home. He made his way to the attic. And in that dark, confined space he took a blade and calmly sliced into his armpit. Death came quickly for John McInnes. By his own hand he was at last freed from his torment. He was 41.

The next morning at just after 10.15 McInnes' limp frame was discovered. Dr Katherine Miller examined the body.

On the death certificate lodged at the nearby village of Strathaven, Dr Miller identified the cause of death.

McInnes had haemorrhaged after cutting the brachial artery in his armpit. His brother Hector registered the death.

A few days later McInnes made what most believed would be his last journey. His coffin was driven to St Ninians cemetery, just outside the village. He was laid to rest in the same lair as his father who was buried there 26 years earlier.

McInnes' mother was also buried in that same grave when she died aged 91 in 1987. On the headstone are inscribed three simple words - TILL HE COME - a reference to the Resurrection and the Lord's supper from the Corinthians, McInnes' favourite and often-quoted part of the Bible.

Sixteen years later John Irvine McInnes rose again to face HIS final judgment. In his village he had not been forgotten and now he will be forever remembered for a very different reason.

Chrissie Richardson, an 83-year-old, worshipped alongside the McInnes family. She went to the same Gospel Hall in Hill Road in Stonehouse where the Brethren gathered. She still attends the Brethren hall nearest to Stonehouse - at Larkhall. She knew John - she called him Irvine - and the rest of his family well. She is well known in the village.

She reflected: "They were a very well respected family in the village. His mother was a very nice woman. The whole family went to the same Hall. He turned to drink. It was a real shame for his mum. It was a real disappointment for her. He just seemed to become depressed with the life he was living and tried to take his own three times before he succeeded.

I don't know why he turned against the Church. It was a very sad affair when he did.

"BUT GOD IS HIS JUDGE. IF HE WAS A MURDERER, HE WILL BE PUNISHED. AS A CHRISTIAN HE WILL BE PUNISHED, NOT IN THIS LIFE BUT IN THE AFTERLIFE."

*Murder victim: Pat Docker*

*Murder victim: Helen Puttock*

*Murder victim: Jemima "Mima" McDonald*

*Pathologist Dr Marie Cassidy changing into
protective overalls at the exhumation of John McInnes*

*Where John McInnes took his life:
26 Queen Street, Stonehouse*

*John McInnes' drinking den:*
*The Old Ship Inn, Stonehouse*

*Aerial view of Stonehouse*

*Graveside vigil: George Puttock mourns his wife Helen*

*Army friend of John McInnes: William Sloan*

*Endless quest: Policeman Joe Beattie at Barrowland*

*Unearthed: McInnes is taken from the grave*

**Extract of an entry in a REGISTER of DEATHS**     **DE** 1216882

*Registration of Births, Deaths and Marriages (Scotland) Act 1965*

| District No. | 579 | Year | 1980 | Entry No. | 44 |
|---|---|---|---|---|---|

Death registered in the district of    Strathaven

| 1 Surname | McINNES | | 2 Sex |
|---|---|---|---|
| Name(s) | John Irvine | | M |

| 3 Occupation | Furniture Salesman |
|---|---|

| 4 Marital status | Divorced | 5 Date of birth | Year 1938 | Month 9 | Day 10 | 6 Age | 41 years |
|---|---|---|---|---|---|---|---|

7 Name(s), surname and occupation of spouse(s)
Helen Russell

8 When and where died    Found dead    19 80 April Thirtieth    1016 hours
26 Queen Street, Stonehouse

9 Usual residence (if different from 8 above)
—————————

| 10 Name(s), surname and occupation of father | 11 Name(s), surname(s) and maiden surname of mother |
|---|---|
| Robert Samson McInnes | Elizabeth McInnes |
| Nurseryman | m.s. Irvine |
| (Deceased) | |

12 Cause of death
I (a)    Haemorrhage

(b)    Laceration of Brachial Artery

(c)

II

Certifying registered medical practitioner    Katherine M. Miller

13 Informant's signature, qualification and address    (Signed)    Hector I McInnes  –  Brother
155 Murray Drive, Stonehouse

| 14 When registered | Year 19 80 | Month 5 | Day 1 | 15 (Signed) | W.R. Cunningham | Registrar |
|---|---|---|---|---|---|---|

16

Extracted from the Register of Deaths for the District of    Strathaven

on    24th January, 1997    *Jean Robertson*    asst Registrar

*John McInnes' death certificate*

*The grave of John McInnes*

# CHAPTER SIX

## WHERE ARE YOU BIBLE JOHN?

*"There is no peace, saith the Lord, unto the wicked."*
Isaiah 48:22

DETECTIVES had a trump card in the hunt for Bible John. They had a witness. Jeannie Williams was a typical hard-working Glesga' woman in the late 1960s. She lived for her kids and worked diligently to provide for them. She didn't want much more from life, perhaps a bit more money every week. That would certainly make things easier. But she enjoyed good health and the children were happy.

But this ordinary, plain-featured woman was unwillingly thrust headlong into the biggest manhunt in Scottish criminal history. She had SEEN Bible John. She'd spent an evening with her sister Helen Puttock in his company. She'd shared a taxi with him. She casually chatted to the man who callously snuffed out her little sister's life. To the police she was vital.

SHE WAS THEIR MAIN HOPE OF CATCHING A KILLER.

A pattern had emerged that indicated the grim handiwork of the same psychopathic monster. Pat

Docker . . . Mima McDonald . . . Helen Puttock. All slaughtered by the same man. Although they steadfastly refused to admit it publicly, the police believed they had a serial killer on the loose in Glasgow. They wanted him caught - and quick. There were striking similarities between the murders of these three ordinary women.

They were ALL married. They had ALL been escorted home by a mystery man moments after midnight. They had ALL been to the Barrowland ballroom on the night they died. They were ALL out for a night on the town, without their regular partners or husbands. They had ALL been strangled with their own tights.

AND, PERHAPS MOST CHILLING OF ALL, THEY WERE ALL HAVING THEIR PERIOD THE WEEK THEY WERE KILLED.

The discovery of Helen Puttock's body in that muddy back court yards from her home was the catalyst for a manhunt of staggering proportions.

IT WAS A MANHUNT WHICH WAS TO LAST 27 YEARS.

Jeannie was struggling to come to terms with her sister's murder. The tears came easily. She and Helen had been close. Her death, and the horrific circumstances surrounding it, were a constant ache in her heart. She couldn't help blaming herself. If only she'd stayed with Helen in the taxi that night. They could have dropped off "Strange John" somewhere - or got shot of him earlier at the Barrowland. Then all this wouldn't have happened. Jeannie was a tormented woman.

Detective Superintendent Joe Beattie was a fighter pilot during the war. He joined the police in 1945, working his way rapidly through the ranks. He was a popular boss with the hard-bitten detectives who worked out of Marine HQ in Glasgow's Partick area. But despite all his experience, the task he was about to perform was never easy.

Joe Beattie knocked on Jeannie Williams' front door. He'd discovered from talking to George Puttock that she had been out at the dancing with Helen at the Barrowland the previous night. Jeannie, still recovering from her late night, was smiling when she opened the door. But she knew immediately something was wrong. The general demeanour of the sombre-looking man standing on her welcome mat gave the game away. She sobbed quietly as Joe Beattie told her that her sister was dead.

Joe Beattie and Jeannie Williams were to speak again many times over the next few years.

George Puttock was quickly eliminated as a suspect. He was ruled out mainly because of Jeannie's detailed account of the sisters' night at the Barrowland. Joe Beattie listened intently as he heard about the man in the Italian suit who shared a taxi ride with Helen and Jeannie. There was no doubt he was the man they were after.

There was no mistaking the pressure each new day brought for Joe Beattie and his 100-strong team of tireless detectives. Things weren't going well. Although the response from newspaper appeals was good, and a lot of information had been gathered, the round-the-clock search on leads disappointingly came to nothing.

Soon after the Puttock murder, the Crown Office in Edinburgh, perhaps mindful of the possible link with the killings of Pat Docker and Mima McDonald, issued what is still today one of the most detailed descriptions of a wanted man ever released to the media. It was based on the recollections of Jeannie Williams from that fateful night. The description was issued by CID boss Detective Chief Superintendent Elphinstone "Elphie" Dalglish. His words painted a vivid picture of a killer. The public appeal was carried on the front pages of most of Scotland's newspapers. It read:

"He is 25 to 30, 5ft 10in to 6ft in height and of medium build. Light auburn, reddish hair, brushed to the right. He has blue-grey eyes and nice straight teeth. But one tooth on the right upper overlaps the next. He has fine features and is generally of a smart, modern appearance. This man was known to have been dressed in a brownish flecked, single-breasted suit with high lapels. His brownish coat - tweed or gabardine - was worn knee-length.

"His wrist watch has a military-style strap (a thick strap with a thinner strap linked through it.) He may smoke Embassy tipped cigarettes and goes to the Barrowland Ballroom. He is thought to be called by his Christian name of John. He may speak of having a strict upbringing and make references to the Bible.

"This man is quite well-spoken, probably with a Glasgow accent. There may be marks on his face and hands." It was the first time since the murder of Pat Docker back in February 1968 that police had been able to put out such a detailed description. Officially, Joe Beattie refused to say there was definitely a link between the Puttock, Docker and McDonald killings, but secretly every CID officer believed they were looking for a triple killer.

They didn't know it at the time, but police really started the Bible John hunt when Pat Docker's naked body was found in that lonely lane in Carmichael Place, Langside, Glasgow, in February 1968. They weren't to know then that the hunt would continue until 1996.

The first people to be questioned by police were Pat's heartbroken mum and dad. John Wilson and his wife told detectives everything they knew about their daughter - her habits her lifestyle. They were desperate to help in any way they could.

Police issued a picture of Pat. Her youthful face beamed out from the nation's front pages. But, underneath, the caption tragically read "Pat Docker . . . murder victim." Detectives also released a picture of a policewoman wearing the same type of clothing that Pat wore the night she died - a yellow crocheted mini dress with a lace pattern design, a fur fabric duffel coat with a hood and brown strapped shoes. Twelve days after her death police revealed they wanted to speak to a man with bruised or cut knuckles. Detective Chief Superintendent Dalglish, said: "The nature of the dead girl's injuries suggests that the assailant may be cut or bruised in the knuckle area of the hand."

The police chief appealed to anyone who was at the dance hall that night to come forward with information.

It was now into March and, in their desperate efforts to crack the Docker case, detectives had interviewed more than 700 of the city's 1300 taxi drivers. It was still a mystery how she'd travelled back to her home area in the Battlefield area of Glasgow that night. The police hoped the key to the riddle lay with the cabbies.

Week after week, police were on dance hall duty. It was thought Pat had gone to the Majestic for her night out - she'd told her parents that's where she was headed. But it was later established after a tip-off that Pat had been dancing the night away at the Barrowland - not the Majestic. Hours of police time had been wasted. The police had been asking questions at the wrong dance hall!

Detectives began the laborious task of trying to track down and interview the hundreds of people who frequented the dance hall. The job was made even harder because of the false alarm over the Majestic. The trail had gone cold. Two weeks after her brutal slaying, The Daily Record distributed posters showing Pat's picture to every newsagent in the Langside area of Glasgow.

THE INQUIRY HAD TO START AGAIN FROM SCRATCH.

Police frogmen looking for Pat Docker's missing clothes discovered her handbag and part of the casing for her watch during a five-hour search of the River Cart near where the tragic nurse's nude body was discovered. But the find was no real help to the police. They still couldn't track down her clothing. They needed to examine what Pat had been wearing that night. That was vital in the hunt for her killer.

Then, suddenly, police thought they had made a breakthrough in the baffling case. Details of a letter, posted in the north of England, were released to the press. The writer, a woman who was probably in Glasgow city centre on the night of the killing, may know the identity of the murderer, claimed police. The woman sent the anonymous letter to George Brownlie, the Detective Chief Inspector in charge of the city's Southern Division. At the time the police said the information in the letter was "vital" to their inquiries. They appealed for the woman to come forward. But she never did. Another blank.

At a press conference, police said they wanted to contact the driver of a Morris 1000 Traveller who pulled up at a bus stop in Langside Avenue on the night of the murder. They also hoped to track down a couple seen in a white Ford Consul. They eventually came forward and were eliminated from the inquiry - another dead end for the hard-working police team. Gradually fewer and fewer people came forward with information. The phone calls to the specially set-up murder room became less frequent; the sightings of Pat Docker that fateful night, fewer. The trail had gone cold.

The Pat Docker murder files had been gathering dust for some 18 months when Mima McDonald's partly-clothed body was found lying sprawled on the floor of a derelict ground-floor flat. Glasgow's murder squad, led by Detective Chief Superintendent Tom Goodall, led a 100-strong team of detectives in the hunt for the sadistic killer of the pretty mum-of-three. There was one chilling fact which immediately jumped out of this new inquiry. Like Pat Docker, Mima had also been to the Barrowland.

As if in a carbon copy of the Docker inquiry, police flooded the dance hall in a bid to track down anyone who might have seen Mima that night. They even flashed the 32-year-old mum's picture on a huge screen at the popular hall a week after the killing. It was a haunting and sobering image for the normally boisterous Barrowland crowd. The music stopped and an eerie hush fell over the dancers. Nobody went home alone that night.

Detectives had a new problem - a hangover from the Pat Docker case. The Barrowland crowd, who may have been able to give police the vital breakthrough, were reluctant to come forward. Many men hadn't told their wives they were going out dancing that night. They were supposed to be in the pub at the time with their mates. Nipping off to the dance halls, especially on over-25s Thursday nights, was a source of excitement for these likely lads. They were literally flirting with danger, but it was always worth the risk. But there was no way they were admitting anything to the police.

Detectives, disappointed by the lack of lines of enquiry, decided to stage a reconstruction of Mima's last movements. They retraced - with the limited knowledge they had - Mima's walk to death. A policewoman, dressed in a dark pinafore and brown coat, was chosen to follow Mima's route home from the Barrowland, along London Road and into Mackeith Street, Bridgeton. Detectives hoped the re-enactment might just jog somebody's memory. Somebody must have seen something that night. They asked people to dig deep into their memory banks. They needed a break. Detective Chief Superintendent Goodall appealed: "We feel someone must have seen this girl walking from the dance hall. We know she was seen in the company of a man. There were many people about that night." The strategy worked. Two people did come forward with vital clues. One man said he'd seen Mima and a red-haired man sitting together in a pub, and a woman claimed she spotted her sitting with a man on a couch at the Barrowland. From their eye-witness accounts, police started to piece together a detailed description of her killer.

Based on the pair's recollections, police then took an unprecedented step, and, in doing so, forever committed the Mima McDonald case to the annals of Scottish legal history. Detectives applied to the procurator-fiscal and the Crown Office for permission to release an identikit picture of the man they were looking for. It was the first time in a Scottish murder inquiry that this step had been taken. The necessary legal hurdles were cleared and the first image of Bible John was drawn by Glasgow School of Art Registrar Lennox Paterson. His drawing was released to the Scottish newspapers. At last police had something tangible - something to show the public in their weary door-to-door treks around Glasgow.

Two months after Mima's death, her sister Jean offered a £100 reward to try and spark the public into action. She told reporters: "This £100 may just be enough to make someone come forward and give the police the vital clue they need. The money comes from myself, three sisters and three brothers. We know it will not bring Mima back, but if the man responsible is caught, it may save the life of some other poor woman."

It was a brave sentiment, but tragically unproductive. There was to be a third murder only eight weeks later.

Meanwhile police officers - male and female - put on their dancing gear again and went on late-night patrol at the Barrowland in the hope that the murderer of Mima McDonald and Pat Docker would return to his killing fields. They were certain he still frequented the dance hall. They prayed he would slip-up - perhaps a loose word after the drink had started to take effect would do it, or a tell-tale remark during a slow dance. The breakthrough the police hoped and worked tirelessly for never came. Mima's killer was never snared, and now police had two unsolved Barrowland murders on their files. They couldn't help thinking the unthinkable. When would this maniac strike again?

They had not long to wait. Helen Puttock went to the dancing with her sister Jeannie Williams. Jeannie got home safely. Helen was never seen alive again.

Superintendent Joe Beattie was seeing a lot of Jeannie Williams. Incredibly, she attended 300 identity parades, desperately looking for the man she and her sister had shared a taxi with. The strange man who quoted the Bible at her. The man she and the police believed so

81

cruelly ended her lovely sister's life. But he was proving to be as elusive as he was charming on that night at the Barrowland. Often Jeannie would get a call at her work at McLaren Controls in West Street asking her to "come down to the station". She never complained, but agonisingly, she was never able to pick out anyone who fitted the bill exactly. It was frustrating for her and the police. She'd seen this man, she'd seen him up close, but on a night out when you are enjoying yourself, when you've had a couple of drinks, you don't pay THAT much attention to detail. Joe Beattie even wanted to hypnotise Jeannie, but the Crown Office frowned upon the idea. Any recollections recounted during hypnosis wouldn't be admissible in a court of law.

During those early weeks of the investigation, Jeannie was to cast her eyes over hundreds of suspects. Many of the men looked like the killer, but she couldn't be sure. She went over that night again and again in her head, desperate to remember a face, a feature - something she'd maybe missed before. But it was no use. After a while all the men on the ID parades began to look the same. Every new line-up brought fresh frustration.

Jeannie was finding it so difficult to point her finger at the man she believed had killed Helen that detectives came up with a new tactic. They asked her to grade the suspects in percentage terms on physical likeness to the man in the taxi. Some ratings were in the high 90s.

Jeannie didn't know it then, but one of the men staring back at her during one of the early parades was John Irvine McInnes . . .

The Puttock case brought with it the birth of the name Bible John in the newspapers, and it immediately captured the public's imagination. Everyone suddenly turned into amateur supersleuths, suspecting their neighbours, their friends - even members of their own family. "I've just seen Bible John," was the familiar phone call to detectives. A fresh identikit picture was released, based on Jeannie's recollection of the murder night. The new picture was uncannily close to Lennox Paterson's drawing produced for the Mima McDonald case. Detectives spared no efforts to make sure the new image was as accurate as possible. To get the exact colour of his hair, they chased, caught and snipped hair from a dog. The identikit - the first one carrying the name Bible John - was made into posters by a number of newspapers. His evil eyes seemed to stare out from every shop, police station and office building. Even today those who were children at the time of the inquiry remember that first image carrying the name Bible John. Every day his face struck a chill into the heart of a nation.

The Helen Puttock inquiry was a mammoth task in police terms and one of the most expensive in history. Officers didn't see their families for days on end. Marriages were wrecked as detectives grew determined to be the one who would snare Bible John. Every angle was covered - or so they thought. After the release of the identikit picture the "sightings" came in thick and fast. In the first year of the Puttock inquiry, 4,300 people said they had seen the killer. The specially set up murder room had become a mountain of paperwork - statements, clues and documentation. Information came from all over the world. Everyone, it seemed had seen Bible John somewhere. One man, who resembled the identikit picture, became upset when work mates teased him about it. His wife began to tease him too. They had a violent row and she left him. Ironically, the man was eliminated from the inquiry after one interview.

Fuelled by massive public interest, the scale of the police operation grew at a staggering pace, stretching their resources to the full. Officers visited 453 hairdressers in the hope that the man with the fair-reddish hair was a customer. They spoke to 240 tailors to establish whether they might have sold Bible John his distinctive continental-style suits. At one point police issued a photograph of a jacket in the style worn by the killer on the night of the Puttock murder. Nine hundred and twenty doctors and dentists were also interviewed, the latter because of the belief that Bible John's two front teeth overlapped slightly. Experts at Glasgow Dental School produced a plaster cast of teeth thought to resemble the killer's. They were photographed and copies sent to every dentist's surgery. 5000 suspects were questioned and slowly eliminated one by one. Some had cast-iron alibis and others had physical features which didn't match the profile of the man they wanted. Bible John had boasted to Jeannie and Helen during that ill-fated taxi ride that a cousin had recently had a hole-in-one, so every golf course secretary in Scotland was asked to provide a list of people who had shot an ace.

Because of his short hair, and the fact that the Docker, McDonald and Puttock murders were spread over 20 months, police looked at the possibility that Bible John was a serving soldier or sailor who came home on irregular leave periods. Bible John posters were sent to the crews of Britain's warships, to Army camps and RAF airfields. Because he quoted the Bible to Helen and Jeannie, churches, chapels and other places of worship were visited. The crews of ships berthed in the Clyde around the time of the Puttock murder were checked out as part of the routine investigation. The possibility that Bible John had a mental disorder was investigated.

Officers visited all Glasgow's hospitals to check patient lists. As in the Docker and McDonald cases, police again concentrated their night-time enquiries at the Barrowland. Two in particular visited the dance hall three times a week. In one of the lighter moments during the probe, one male detective said: "We must be the best dancers in the world. We are there twice a week. People must think we are strange. It's the only time I go to the dancing looking for a man."

The Puttock case had become the most thorough murder hunt ever launched in Scotland. A policewoman at Marine Division was employed full-time sending photofit posters to every police station in Britain. Three Army deserters were court martialled after being caught in the Bible John police net. Several men were forced to carry cards with the telephone number of Chief inspector George Lloyd because they'd been reported and brought in to police stations so many times. Carrying the card avoided further arrests.

George Puttock was asked - and agreed - to take part in a historic press conference in Glasgow. It was the first time ever that the husband of a murder victim had appealed publicly for help. George made his emotional plea as he sat in a dusty Glasgow courtroom at a desk normally occupied by lawyers. Facing a battery of pressmen, he spoke about Helen, his children and the mysterious Bible John. In a dramatic statement, the heartbroken husband said: "I'd like to ask this man John to consider me and the two children. This thing has ruined my career. I am a corporal in the Royal Signals, awaiting promotion. I have done 11 years and now I will have to leave. And I've been left with my two children, five-year-old David and baby Michael. Their mother loved the children. So do I and I can't be a weekend father now that they have lost their mother. I hope this appeal will help bring this man to justice."

Anguished George later offered a £200 reward - most of his life savings to help trap the killer. He told reporters: "Everything else has failed so far. The police have worked their guts out, but no-one has so far supplied the clue that will trap this monster." As heartbroken George attended his wife's funeral at Glasgow's Lambhill Cemetery senior CID officers mingled with mourners in the hope that Bible John would turn up.

Police also wanted to trace the man known as Castlemilk John who danced with Jeannie Williams and walked with Helen Puttock and McInnes to a taxi rank after that fateful visit to the Barrowland. Castlemilk John dashed off to get a late-night bus home and was never seen again. Despite countless police pleas the man never came forward - possibly because he hadn't told his wife he was going dancing that night. Later Joe Beattie expressed his regret that the man was never traced. "One of my biggest regrets is that Castlemilk John never came forward. That was a bad break in the investigation. He would have been able to help. He was in Bible John's company that night. And he may have known something about the killer which could have identified him. It is reasonable to assume that during that evening the two men would have exchanged information," said Beattie.

In March, 1970, police accepted a dossier compiled by world-famous Dutch clairvoyant Gerard Croiset who had helped police all over the world in solving countless murder mysteries. Mr Croiset jetted into Glasgow from his home in Utrecht and set to work. He asked for and was given only the minimum details about the case - Helen Puttock's name, age and where her body was found. Then with a pen, the clairvoyant began to make sketches, most of them showing details of an area of Glasgow which he claimed had some connection with the wanted man. He pinpointed shops, giving detailed descriptions of the people working in them. He drew streets, factories, a cinema, a school and a small square surrounded by iron railings. With no prior knowledge he described how Helen Puttock spent her last evening dancing. He described the Barrowland's layout and where she sat with her killer, and he told how she left with other people. He even sketched a rough map of the city and blacked out an area where he thought Bible John could be found. He described Bible John as "a young man, no more than 28, with fairish hair". He said he was keen on body building, "fairly tall and walked erect with shoulders back and chest stuck out." Police were ordered to search buildings, shops, factories, recreation grounds and schools in the South Side of Glasgow which Croiset saw in his mind's eye and sketched on pieces of paper.

Six months later, there was an upsurge in public interest after a BBC Current Account programme. The telephone switchboard at Glasgow's Marine Police Station was jammed with 350 calls shortly after the programme finished at 9pm. The programme ended with a personal appeal to Bible John to give himself up. Presenter Hugh Cochrane said: "If you are out there watching, maybe it is time for you to come out of the glare for your own good."

In 1983, police considered dramatic new evidence after a Glasgow businessman Harry Wylie claimed he knew who Bible John was. At his own expense he hired investigators Bill Blyth and Richard McCue, Scotland's most scrupulous private eye team. Wylie claimed Bible John was an old mate from childhood schooldays. The dossier compiled by the pair named David Henderson who was living in Holland. Wylie first suspected David when he returned from Australia and read a newspaper article recalling the Bible John murders. He took one look at the artist's impression and concluded: "That could be Davie Henderson." Henderson was quizzed and later ruled out by police.

In 1992, the 25 boxes of evidence and statements were dusted down again when pornographic material with religious connotations was found in a house on the outskirts of the city. Another false alarm. Another disappointment.

In 1993, detectives announced the news which was eventually to lead to a breakthrough in the baffling case. They said that the semen stain left behind by Helen Puttock's killer could possibly now be re-examined using pioneering genetic profile techniques. They hoped it was the beginning of the end in the hunt for Scotland's most elusive killer.

It was revealed in the Sunday Mail in December, 1995, that the Bible John case was being actively investigated again. The probe was in full flow. A four-man team based in Partick police station in the heart of Glasgow was asked to pour over huge files relating to the case and check for anything that could finally crack it.

The investigation was led by Chief Inspector Jim McEwan who was relying on the fact that a much greater range of forensic techniques and equipment would be at his disposal. McEwan knew there had been a good DNA analysis from the Helen Puttock case. Her killer had left a semen stain on her clothes during his frenzied sex attack. The detective knew all about the men who had been high on the suspect list. He knew a DNA match from a suspect or one of his relatives could bring him closer to cracking the case.

Two detective constables, William Lindsay and Brian Hughes, were assigned the task of combing through the piles of statements and documents amassed during the early years of the probe. They spent hours chatting with officers, all now retired from the original inquiry. Everything that surfaced was logged onto computer along with the key clues from 26 years ago. The fourth member of the team was crime analyst Susan McHarg.

The task was arduous and time-consuming but they narrowed their new list of suspects down to just 12. Throughout the inquiry the name John Irvine McInnes surfaced again and again. But the police team knew that to nail him once and for all as Bible John they had to get access to his grave. Details of their probe were carefully drafted into a lengthy report sent to the procurator fiscal along with a request for the exhumation of their number one suspect. They had a file full of circumstantial evidence linking him to the Puttock case. On January 27, 1996, Strathclyde Police, Scotland's biggest force, issued a statement confirming the latest developments and the plan for the exhumation. Two days later every newspaper in the land recapped the gruesome tales of Bible John's sadistic activities during the late 1960s and speculated about the outcome. A DNA match would be the icing on the cake.

They also had a plaster cast made in 1969 of a bite mark found on Helen Puttock's body. Police wanted to check whether McInnes' teeth matched the impression.

The search for that DNA match led them to Stonehouse Cemetery on February 1, 1996. And it was a blonde woman in the cemetery on that winter's morning who would play a key role in finding that final clue.

She was Marie Cassidy, a highly-respected pathologist, charged with the task of sifting through the bone, skin and remnants of his coffin that had been lowered into the grave 16 years before. A day earlier she'd spoken for the first time about her task - certain the tests would confirm once and for all the identity of Bible John. She calmly spoke of the prospect of the job and said: "Death is my job. I deal with it and see it first-hand every day."

A police video team recorded every single second of that historic and significant morning, the cameraman capturing images of each person taking part and every stage of the gruesome task. A helicopter, chartered by a newspaper, hovered above, taking in a bird's eye view of the scene.

A 60-strong army of press had turned up. They'd learned about the police plans just three days earlier. No-one wanted to miss the most important twist in the saga for years. Some had been there since 3am - camping out in sleeping bags, reclined in their cars.

The police had asked for the exhumation to be carried out with respect and dignity. A special plea was issued to the public - "Keep away". The 5,000 or so residents of Stonehouse, shocked by the revelations, didn't rush to the cemetery. They were uncomfortable about this sudden invasion and intrusion on their doorstep.

A man armed with his home video camera appeared - he lived on a neighbouring farm and the police knew of his presence. But three strangers - a bearded man with two middle-aged women - turned up, at first refusing to explain their involvement, a situation which only served to fuel the journalists' speculation that they were members of McInnes' family.

The women walked away as the man fielded question after question - almost revelling in the attention.

Eventually he promised: "We'll make a statement when we're ready." Five minutes later they were chatting away at an impromptu press conference by the graveyard gates. Reporters scribbled frantically and cameras clicked.

The man - describing himself as a professional psychic who earned his living by using his "power" - claimed he had been contacted by Helen Puttock. He claimed they'd kept in touch for 22 years. The man emphatically stated that McInnes wasn't the real Bible John and that his woman from beyond claimed her killer was another man - at that time still alive and living nearby in Motherwell. He was, according to the man who boasted 40 years of psychic involvement, working in the field of education.

But his colleague, a stout, heavily made-up woman dressed in black leggings and a short, dark-coloured jacket, offered a different story to the assembled press-pack. Boasting of her psychic powers, she claimed she was very much aware of John McInnes' torment since he'd taken his own life. She claimed he was suffering "like the fires of hell" . She added that she felt he had been involved in at least a couple of murders.

But both agreed on one point. They were opposed to the exhumation. The man said: "I don't see what the purpose of it all is. What is it going to serve? I don't think we should be pursuing people beyond the grave. It's going against natural law."

Indeed the exhumation sparked a big row. Less than a week later, an MP echoed the psychics' comments, slamming the exhumation and the police role in it as a publicity stunt. The Labour Party's John McAllion accused Strathclyde Police of wasting scarce cash. But his remarks were rejected by the police. Their spokesman emphasised: "We are talking about unsolved murder inquiries which never close. If fresh evidence comes to light, we're duty bound to follow it up."

And, in what then became a cross-party political row, the Conservative's Scottish chairman Sir Michael Hirst hit back, wondering if Mr McAllion had taken leave of his senses and said: "The families of these victims, whose murders have never been solved will, of course, want the police to get to the bottom of it. The police do a wonderful job and deserve public support, not carping from mean-minded politicians."

On that bleak winter morning with the digging well underway, the police and reporters knew there was good reason to have this grave opened up. The older members of the journalistic pack, who had covered the murders, flicked through their original cuttings, frantically checking over details for their stories. To a captive audience, two of the hacks swapped tales, reliving their recollections often starting with the phrase: "When I . . ." or "I remember . . ."

The new faces among the journalists listened intently, storing away every detail in their quest to get to grips with the story that, in Scotland, had been dubbed the crime of the century. Many hadn't even been born when Bible John posters stared from every police station in the land at the height of the probe into the savage killings. One young female journalist boasted to an older colleague: "My mother covered this case at the time!"

Almost 30 years after his last murder the Scottish press was again dominated by the Bible John saga. Plenty of other things were happening to hit the headlines. The so-called Dukegate scandal revealing details of a mobile phone call between Prince Philip and close family friend, Lady Penny Romsey, had been filling columns of national papers. Another newspaper story told how a bride's big day was ruined when a spurned ex-friend cancelled her wedding limos. In Stonehouse these and other stories were of little or no consequence as concentration zeroed in on the police and their delicate operation.

At a briefing for the huge pack of newspaper, radio and TV journalists the question was asked: "Will they use a drill to open up the grave?" The police press spokesman breathed in deeply and said: "Spades, they'll use spades. There's about half a dozen officers involved." But the ground was solid and the drill was the only fast way to crack open a site that had been snow-covered for days and hardened by some of the most extreme temperatures experienced in Scotland for years.

By 9.15 that morning, the graveyard was cleared of everyone apart from the police and council officials. Marie Cassidy was joined by an eminent Scots pathologist Professor Anthony Basuttil of Edinburgh University and a member of Scotland's procurator fiscal service - the court prosecutors - as the digging continued. Chief Superintendent James Young oversaw the entire operation. A solicitor, representing McInnes' family, watched every step of the proceedings. This was no ordinary exhumation. It was believed to be the first exhumation in Scotland in recent times to be carried out as part of a murder investigation. The pressmen moved outside the gates, the waiting game underway. A couple of reporters, better prepared than others, sipped at steaming cups of soup and coffee. Others chattered away on their mobile telephones, keeping news desks and picture desks fully updated on the big story.

It was then that Marie Cassidy and her colleague Janet McFarlane moved in to oversee the delicate exhumation before the careful DNA analysis and exhaustive tests. Nearly six months after John Irvine McInnes' remains were exhumed officers completed a report for the procurator fiscal.

Detective Superintendent Joe Beattie, now retired, keeps poor health at his home in Bearsden just outside the city. But his words uttered years after the Bible John trail had gone stone cold still stick in the throat:

"WE NEVER EVEN GOT A SNIFF AT HIM. WE MUST HAVE MISSED HIM RIGHT AT THE START."

# CHAPTER SEVEN

## THE VILLAGE OF SECRETS

*"His blood be on us, and on our children.."*
Matthew 27:24-25

NOTHING much ever happened in Stonehouse. A small village in the heart of the Lanarkshire countryside, it boasts a people proud of their working-class roots with dirt under their fingernails and real hearts of gold. Historically, its streets were trodden by generations of weavers and miners following in the footsteps of ancestors stretching back to Roman times. It was a solid community with little or no secrets, a typical village where everyone knew a great deal about everyone else's business. People didn't go out of their way to court publicity - Stonehouse is not really that sort of place.

The pubs buzzed with everyday village gossip. They were the community's focal points, the places where everyday chit-chat could be swapped and, inevitably, exaggerated.

The village's short entry in an old Scottish Gazetteer boasted the local railway station as its only place of interest. Forever shadowed by the nearby larger industrial towns of Hamilton and Motherwell, Stonehouse was very much the poor relation in Lanarkshire - almost forgotten once the busy A74/ M74 sliced the umbilical cord which connected it with the rest of the county. Life in Stonehouse was lived at a slow pace in the 1950s and 1960s with the main highlight each year being the village gala day. Even today that long-awaited June day sees most of the inhabitants turn out in their finery to watch the snake-like procession of brightly-decorated floats, the gala queen crowning ceremony and various side shows and attractions. Indeed it was the gala day that once gave Stonehouse its only real taste of publicity . . . and the rest of Scotland a chuckle. As if they'd had some kind of communal rush of blood to the head, gala day organisers hatched the idea of inviting golden oldie Hollywood actress Zsa Zsa Gabor to be their patron. In the end she didn't turn up - and, after a few columns of newspaper attention, Stonehouse's anonymity was restored.

But in 1996 everything changed - forever. The village became synonymous with MURDER.

OVERNIGHT, STONEHOUSE HAD ITS NAME CARVED ON BRITAIN'S BLOOD-STAINED MAP OF NOTORIETY.

Never again will this once-peaceful community be allowed to return to normality.

In February, 1996, John McInnes, the former furniture salesman's name became inextricably linked with Scotland's most baffling murder mystery.

Serial killer - the criminologist's term for murderers with a blood lust that has to be satisfied over and over again - was coined by American FBI man, Robert Ressler, in the mid-1980s. He used it to describe the "thrill-killer" who carried on murdering until caught. Childhood abuse, an unhappy family life and personality flaws, such as acute shyness, are often cited as factors in the make-up of the mass murderer.

Many experts believe the one common factor which turns a seemingly ordinary man into a monster is SEX. Those who sat through the trial of Scotland's mass killer Peter Manuel cannot possibly forget the unhealthy undercurrent to the evidence. Forensic evidence showed him to be a sexually impotent psychopath, unable to form relationships with women. He only found a sick satisfaction after killing, a feeling of "superiority", by exercising the power of life and death.

Crime expert Colin Wilson once gave a chilling diagnosis of what goes wrong in the mind of a killer:

" The serial killer has discovered a drug that frees him from the miseries and inadequacies of his life. Unfortunately it can become a terrifyingly addictive drug . . . by comparison, heroin is harmless."

Bible John's addiction to death and its aftermath lasted for years. But he always managed to stay one step ahead of the police. Most murderers are quickly caught, but in the case of Bible John it was different. It was very different. For almost 10,000 days the identity of the sex killer remained unknown. The police probe into the murders of Pat Docker, Mima McDonald and Helen Puttock was not short of enthusiasm, dedication and commitment. In retrospect it lacked the one vital ingredient to snare a killer - a lucky break.

The one person who did get that lucky break was Bible John. In the majority of murder cases the guilty person is interviewed by police within the first 48 hours. In the Puttock probe Bible John even stood face-to-face with the one main witness who could be certain of the killer's identity. She walked past him, failing to pick him out of a line-up. How he must have cherished that moment, smiling inwardly. They'd missed him. He'd got away with it.

He must have smiled again as he walked past police stations, shops and offices displaying the now famous Bible John Wanted posters. How he must have thought the image staring out was like looking in a mirror. How he must have puzzled endlessly over why no-one could spot the resemblance, the similarity around the eyes and that distinctive curve of the lips. He must have sneered when he picked up newspapers over the years and read about the Barrowland dance hall murders and saw the creation of the monster that was Bible John. His creation.

He must have smirked whenever the name of Detective Superintendent Joe Beattie was mentioned. Beattie led the huge manhunt which failed to track down Bible John. And he must have seen the humour as the highly-respected police chief's officers put their marriages at stake to go on "dance hall duty" at the Barrowland. He may even have danced beside them. He had a good laugh at them all. Joe Beattie dedicated a huge chunk of his life to capturing a maniac. One of his many quotes became a classic from the Bible John investigation. Beattie, reflecting during a retirement dogged by ill-health, said: "We never even got a sniff at him. We must have missed him right at the start, and yet we knew almost everything about him."

There can be no more frustrating and agonising situation for a top police officer than when a murder file remains unsolved. Joe Beattie believed he would crack the Puttock case within the first few weeks. After all the police knew so much about the killer. They had to get their man. The public had been more than willing to help. As it turned out it needed advanced forensic science - not available in Beattie's era - to help close the file on Bible John.

The Bible John killings in the late 1960s stand in a

class of their own in a city where once the knuckle-duster and the razor were king, but now the knife and the gun rule.

The Bible John case cannot be easily categorised. These killings weren't the results of pub arguments, domestic disputes or scraps in the street. They were pre-meditated, callous and brutal and all had a bizarre twist. Each of his known victims had been menstruating. In one case he left the poor woman's soiled sanitary towel tucked under her armpit. It was a sickeningly bizarre act. Nobody could understand or even guess at its significance. Was it then just coincidence that 12 years later when McInnes let HIS life-blood slowly drain away, he sliced into a main artery under his own armpit?

Was Bible John a man obsessed by the Biblical writings of Leviticus which said that a menstruating woman is "unclean"? Was he the son of a domineering mother? Was there perhaps a feminine streak to his nature which instinctively drew him and allowed him to "sense" women he was certain were having their periods? Why did he target married women, out on their own for a night of fun at the dancing? Why did he use items of their own clothing to squeeze the very last breath from their limp bodies? Did he snap when he realised his desire for sex with his chosen women had been thwarted? Had his conscience at last caught up with him, swamping and tormenting him to that point where he could no longer cope? There will never be definite answers to these questions.

Throughout the last 27 years hundreds of thousands of words have been penned about Bible John. The mystery has been the subject of countless radio and TV programmes. Newspaper and magazine articles all round the world have charted the saga and the incredible hunt, updating whenever there was any new twist or development. A generation of children grew up learning about the legend that dominated their parents' earlier years. And as these children matured so too have medical science and police forensic techniques developed. And it was science and its appliance in crime detection that was used to finally try and snare Bible John.

When McInnes ended his life in 1980 in the attic of his mother's home, he thought he could find everlasting peace in his grave in the isolated Stonehouse Cemetery.

Sixteen years later his rest was disturbed and a question mark placed over his name.

# CHAPTER EIGHT

## A KILLER'S CALLING CARD

*"The tree is known by his fruit..."*
Matthew 12:33

AT a Home Office forensic science lab a placard pinned on a door proclaims: "BY THEIR DNA SO SHALL YE KNOW THEM." To dedicated researchers it's not without humour, a light-hearted flirtation with a science that normally throws up everything but laughs. To killers at large it's a chilling warning that the hunt won't back down. DNA - or genetic profiling - is for today's police what fingerprints were for Dixon of Dock Green, TV's classic cop series which spanned the 1950s, 1960s and 1970s.

Watch any police drama on television and you'll see it . . . The moment that every murder squad detective dreads: when the trail goes cold, the file is stamped unsolved and locked away. Nowadays, thankfully, there are fewer such files.

Police investigation techniques have come a long, long way since the late 1960s. The progress of forensic science both in the UK and the USA has given detectives a huge helping hand in cracking what on the face of things, looks like the uncrackable. A most important key to probing modern crimes is now considered to be DNA matching - where a "genetic fingerprint" can be linked from a suspect to what may be considered the tiniest, most insignificant piece of hair, skin or moisture left on a victim or at the scene of crime. Everybody has DNA - it's in our genes - and the scientists have devised sophisticated methods of building up a picture which is something akin to a supermarket bar-code specific to every individual. It has been argued that unlike real fingerprints, DNA profiles are not unique to individuals. Since its development and increased usage in many cases the science has attracted its critics, unhappy about the accuracy. Defence lawyers attempt to convince juries to disregard it. Coupled with other clues, however, they can prove to be vital in tracking down killers. DNA profiling has been used in hundreds of thousands of cases world-wide since the mid-1980s. Had DNA been available in the late 1960s and early 1970s, the Bible John case doubtlessly would have been solved, the killer brought to justice and the files closed.

Those involved in the Bible John cases were reluctant to admit defeat. The disturbing knowledge that any killer could be walking around free brings torment to the police and haunts the families of the victims.

The man who was the real Bible John could never have imagined the great technological advances of the future. He believed he'd outfoxed some of the best detective minds in the land. The nickname he earned appeared and re-appeared in newspapers, magazines and other books on famous crimes. Fingerprints - hundreds of them - were taken during the early years of the Bible John murder probe. It was normal police practice. Suspects pulled in for questioning were put through the short identification process that is often so crucial in nailing criminals. But it was clear that it would take more, much more, than a fingerprint match to solve the murder mysteries.

As the years have progressed so has the genetic fingerprinting technique. Once the forensic expert needed a blood stain or body fluid sample at least the size of a 5p coin. Now only tiny scraps of human material can be sufficient. It was said that the newer methods could even solve the most notorious unsolved case in British history - who was Jack the Ripper? A stain on the victim and a DNA sample from a suspect might have been enough to catch that legendary murderer. In Scotland detectives first used the DNA technique in 1989. Lothian and Borders Police probing the double killings of two young women in a case dubbed the World's End murders. Christine Eadie and Helen Scott were murdered in October 1977 after leaving the World's End pub in the High Street, right in the heart of Edinburgh. At the time of writing the case has still not been solved. The girls, both 17, were friends, and both from the same area of the city. They were seen leaving the pub with two men. The next day Christine was found naked near North Berwick in East Lothian. Helen was found a few hours later in a field, partially clothed.

Over the years samples have been checked using DNA and rechecked as the technology advances. Police insiders revealed that DNA tests have been used to eliminate people from the inquiry but as a result of some of the tests others have come into the frame as possible suspects. The Edinburgh detectives haven't lost heart. One said: "In that time we haven't produced any results which have allowed us to identify the murderer or murderers.

"Nevertheless the forensic work carried out so far has produced information which may prove to be of value in the future and of course we will continue to harness further technological advances to assist our inquiries."

It's certainly true to say that not every case is suitable for the DNA test technology, but that mode of investigation is applicable in crimes where sexual assault, rape and violent physical attack are involved. The closer the contact by the perpetrator the more likely the chance that the DNA hit will prove successful.

Helen Puttock's pair of brown nylons had been guarded like the Crown Jewels since her death. Carefully preserved and protected from the elements, the garment was key evidence in one of the most baffling cases ever in Scotland. On that night of horror in 1969 Helen Puttock's killer sadistically forced the last breath from her body, wrapping the garment tightly around her neck. But it wasn't just the piece of clothing that proved to be so vital. When the detectives had the garment carefully analysed experts pinpointed a small stain. It was a semen stain. In DNA terms, the man who killed Helen had left a mark as good as his signature. In his lust for blood and his evil crusade against women the killer had effectively left his calling card.

When all these years later police re-examined the files locked away in Partick Police Station in Glasgow they knew exactly what they were working towards. They needed to go over every shred of evidence and, using modern technology, re-evaluate and determine if anything could close the net on the killer. They knew they could secure a DNA sample from a suspect and hopefully match it with the stain on the tights. The DNA hit was in the bag - they just needed to match it up.

The team focused a great deal of attention on John Irvine McInnes. There was, however, a slight complication. He was dead. He'd committed suicide and was buried. They had to go for the next best thing. A relative. The job wasn't going to be easy. But they successfully traced and contacted relatives and obtained DNA swabs, believed to be from his brother, Hector, and sister, Etta, who both still live in the village of Stonehouse where McInnes was buried. The samples were taken away to the police labs and prepared for DNA testing.

It's not a quick process but on this occasion the wait seemed like an eternity. The results were relayed back to the Partick police team at the centre of the fresh investigation. One of the DNA samples from the relatives did match the stain on Helen Puttock's tights. Officers had made a big step forward. The next step forward was even bigger.

They needed to exhume McInnes' remains from their resting place and run the DNA process over a series of samples. They also needed an impression of his teeth. They knew the killer had bitten his victim. The impression could be used to match the bite marks. Only at that stage could they positively confirm what they suspected.

Weeks of laborious DNA testing of McInnes' remains turned quickly into months. Strathclyde police's forensic lab worked day and night to establish a link between McInnes' DNA sample and the semen stain on Helen Puttock's tights. The poor state of his remains gave scientists a major headache, and the police's original estimate of three weeks to complete the tests proved to be wildly off the mark. Police eventually called in expert advice from scientists at the University of Cambridge, and after weeks of pressure from MPs, completed a report for the Lord Advocate.

The Lord Advocate issued a statement on July 4, 1996, which concluded that forensic tests had failed to link McInnes with the semen stain found on Helen Puttock's body. The tests on the bitemark were also inconclusive, said the Lord Advocate. Police also submitted details of circumstantial evidence to the procurator-fiscal, claiming McInnes could be pinpointed at key times during the night of Helen Puttock's murder. But it wasn't enough to finally name Scotland's most notorious and elusive killer.

# CHAPTER NINE

## HOW MANY DID HE KILL?

*"Their bodies are buried in peace; but their name liveth for evermore."*
Ecclesiastes 44:14

THE name Bible John was thrown up time and time again whenever other women were murdered. In many cases it was just pure speculation. Others sparked renewed interest because of the similarities to the Puttock, McDonald and Docker deaths. On occasions, and very much in private, police believed some were simply copycat killings, the work of evil men obsessed by the Bible John case, their perverted, twisted minds looking to him as some sort of cult figure. In some cases, however, the killings were just too similar for comfort. These cases remained unsolved at the time of John Irvine McInnes' body being exhumed. Were they Bible John's victims and just how many did he kill?

The idea of a serial killer at loose in Scotland has provided authors with many a chapter in their crime anthologies. Did he wallow in the notoriety - preferring that to being ignored in his sad, sick existence? Did he relish the idea of going down in the history books as a major criminal and was he obsessed at seeing his cases written about in the pages of newspapers, magazines and books? The revelation of who exactly Bible John was gives the subject a clearer focus but still many questions remain unanswered. Was Bible John capable of more heinous crimes during his life-time? He had been clever enough to avoid arrest once. Indeed he stood in an identity parade and came face to face with a key witness who had seen him with one of his victims. But she passed him by, unable at that time to say he was the guilty man. But did that and his criminal "good luck" simply charge him up to satisfy his hunger for murder again and again?

With the reopening of the Bible John inquiry, detectives - always keen to keep their options open when investigating crimes - looked closely at four other unsolved murder cases.

They kept the similarities of the Puttock, McDonald and Docker cases at the forefront of their crime busting minds. The four victims were all young women who had gone out for the evening. Three were picked up from entertainment venues - just like the original Bible John killings. And all were found dead with their handbags missing - another similarity to the McInnes murders.

Brewery worker Anna Kenny was the first in the new batch of murders. She disappeared on August 5, 1977, after a night out in Glasgow. Anna, 20, and a friend, Wilma Sutherland, had been at the Hurdy Gurdy pub and the pair met two men in the smokey bar. At closing time she left with one of them and headed towards the city's George Square to catch her bus home to the Gorbals area. She was seen walking alone in the Townhead district of Glasgow after midnight and police believe she left her young male companion to hail a taxi. What exactly happened after that point remains a mystery. Who did she meet up with? Where did he take her? She didn't make it home and failed to turn up at her work on the Monday.

Anna's body wasn't discovered until 20 months later - 100 miles from her home. Her remains were found in a remote part of Argyll, a beautiful, desolate piece of the Scottish countryside below a hillside overlooking the Kilbrannan Sound in Kintyre. It was the stuff picture postcards are made of, but on that day it was a scene of horror. Two shepherds stumbled across her makeshift grave. Forensic experts revealed her neck and ankles had been bound.

On October 1, 1977, divorced mum Hilda McAuley Miller went out to the popular Plaza ballroom on the south side of Glasgow. Saturday was the one night of the week she went out while her mother Martha looked after her sons George, 13, and Mark, aged nine. Her last ever night out was with her pals and the group stopped off for a drink at McNee's bar next to the dance hall. She was seen chatting to a man in his 30s. She later danced the Saturday night away.

The following day a group of boys out playing found a female's battered body dumped in a wooded area near a lover's lane in Langbank on the River Clyde in Renfrewshire. The victim had severe head injuries and was strangled and raped. She'd been cast aside like a rag doll into the deep grass. Hilda's mum read of the grim discovery in her newspaper. As she struggled to digest each line she realised she was reading about Hilda. She recognised the description. Weeping and clutching the newspaper, she walked into Maryhill Police headquarters in Glasgow and quietly told the policeman on the counter why she was there.

Later she said: "Hilda only lived for her two sons.

Her only break in the week was her regular Saturday night out with her girlfriends. Hilda never had a boyfriend since her divorce eight years ago. They must get her killer. Hilda never asked for this. If I knew him and could get my hands on him . . ."

Hilda's clothing had been scattered about and her double-breasted light fawn coat, tan platform shoes and handbag were missing. There was no form of identification left at the scene.

One of the problems in the Bible John case was the reluctance of the dance hall people to come forward. Then it was the Barrowland dancers who were not keen to co-operate. This time the Plaza-goers stayed silent. They didn't want their names known. That wall of silence frustrated the police. It protected the men and women who were married and for many out cheating on their partners. As a detective said: "Many are not admitting they were there last week."

In December that year the killer struck again - he had the taste for killing and nothing it seemed would stop him. This time it was a children's nurse Agnes Cooney, 23, from Coatbridge, Lanarkshire, who had gone out for the evening to the Clada Club in Westmoreland Street, a short walk from the Plaza. She'd gone to the popular club to see a pop group. There were about 200 people there that night. In the early hours of the morning she'd left to go home. She was never seen alive again. The man responsible had focused on that same area, disregarding the risk of police attention since the earlier killing.

The next day Agnes' body was found by a farmer in Lanarkshire. John Stewart had been driving his tractor along a lonely road when he spotted her. Hundreds of drivers must have passed the murder spot unaware of the tragedy just 20 yards from the main road. She had been stabbed 26 times. The pathologists revealed she'd died after a violent struggle.

It was officially disclosed that she had been held captive for up to 24 hours before she was stabbed to death. There was no evidence of sexual attack but police considered the motive may have been sexual. Another mysterious twist was the fact that Agnes, a single woman, was found wearing a thin gold band on her wedding finger.

Two years later Mary Gallagher, 17, was found beaten to death in the Springburn district of Glasgow. The background mirrored the previous cases...a planned night out with the girls at the Firhill Social Club in Maryhill. She didn't even get there.

Earlier in the day she had been baby-sitting for a friend. She'd rushed home, had her tea and went to her room to get ready. Mary who worked as a machinist, brushed her short dark hair and changed into a neat outfit of dark velvet jacket, black cord trousers and a pair of ankle-length cowboy style leather boots with three inch heels. They made the diminutive teenager look much taller than her four feet 11 inches. She left her home in Keppochhill and the police believe it was just 15 minutes later that her killer struck. The police believe he had been lurking in a lane, waiting for a woman, any woman. Mary was the unlucky one. He'd marked her down for death for no other reason than that she had walked along a dark lane on her own. Her handbag was missing. Apparently there had been no sexual motive in Mary's murder.

All these cases prompted the police to refer to a report by Dr Robert P. Brittain, a leading consultant psychiatrist, which profiled the mind of a killer. His explosive document gave a fascinating insight into the mind and workings of a beast. The expert had 20 years of interviewing sex killers and detectives believed it would help them pinpoint the maniac. Dr Brittain died in 1971. Here are some of his thoughts:

*"People might think of him as a large, hulking brute, crude, over-sexed, wild-eyed with a history of mental illness - but a sex killer is usually not like this at all. He looks much like other people.*

*"He is usually rather withdrawn, has few friends and usually no close ones. His pursuits are solitary.*

*"Sometimes but by no means always he is recognised by his acquaintances as being strange, off-beat, twisted, a loner, kinky or a weirdie.*

*"He is without remorse of conscience as regards his offences, no matter what the cruelty involved. He is not concerned with the moral implications of his acts and treats them casually.*

*"He is without pity for his victims. He can detach himself from his killings, being aware of them but not emotionally involved. He knows he is responsible for what he has done but refuses to believe it.*

*"After his crimes he will often behave normally, returning home to eat and sleep well.*

*"Intellectually he knows right from wrong but this does not inhibit him.*

*"Such a man very frequently has a strange relationship with his mother, both loving her and hating her.*

*"Often he is known as a particularly devoted son, emotionally very closely bound to her, bringing her gifts to a degree beyond the ordinary.*

*"He's a mother's boy, even when adult.*

*"These men suffer not from a single sexual perversion but from a number.*

"These often require privacy when they are being performed so there may be knowledge that they lock themselves away in rooms for hours, or that they have a shed or other private place where no one else is allowed to enter.

"The murder itself may be very carefully planned and preparations made sometimes even days or weeks ahead.

"He can think it all out very clearly and wait until he finds a suitable time, place and victim and manipulate circumstances to achieve his ends.

"SUCH CAREFUL PLANNING BY AN INTELLIGENT MAN AND WHERE THERE IS LITTLE TO ASSOCIATE THE KILLER WITH HIS VICTIM CAN MAKE HIS DETECTION VERY DIFFICULT.

"At the time of his crime he becomes excited and usually uses more force than is required, merely to kill.

"He is now transformed into a very different person from the shy, timid, withdrawn type he normally appears to his acquaintances.

"His reason is dulled and his sexual drive and desire for power take over control of his actions.

"The sight of suffering can inflame him and his brutality can be increased by the helplessness and fear of his victims.

"They can feel a god-like power and can play with their victims like a cat with a mouse.

"After the crime is completed the murderer may feel relaxed and experience a great relief of tension.

"Sometimes there is a feeling of disappointment as he may find he hasn't achieved the degree of pleasure, excitement and thrill which he anticipated.

"Therefore he can commit murder again in further attempts to gain relief.

"If he does commit further crimes, he tends to be

*reasonably faithful to the methods he has already used.*

*"Given the opportunity, the sadistic murderer is likely to kill again."*

In the case of Bible John a full profile of the man behind the name can never be drawn up. Too many questions remain unanswered. Too many gaps can't be filled. The extent of his terror reign cannot be fully disclosed.

# CHAPTER TEN

## HIS LEGACY OF TEARS

*"For in much wisdom is much grief: and he that increaseth
knowledge increaseth sorrow."*
Ecclesiastes 1:18

The telephone rang in the luxury house in a corner of the globe thousands of miles from Scotland. When she picked up the receiver Ella Thornqvist thought it sounded like a long-distance call. She was used to that. Lorna often called from her home in New Zealand. She recognised her daughter's voice the instant she spoke. But she knew right away there was something different about her tone.

The words she heard next will stay with her for as long as she lives. It was one of those conversations that chills the heart. Each sentence was worse than the one before. Each word hit her like a thunderbolt. Her past came flooding back as she tried to put what she had just been told into some sort of perspective. It wasn't the easiest thing to do.

Ella Thornqvist lives in style in Riyadh in oil-rich Saudi Arabia. It's a world apart from her "old life" in the 1960s when she was married to John McInnes and scraping an existence together in Ayrshire.

Money worries are a thing of the past now. Her new husband Rolfe is a senior executive with a major international company. She's settled well into the tax-free lifestyle enjoyed by many foreigners working in the Middle East. Times are really good now for Ella. Indeed, after she had returned for a brief visit to Scotland one of her relatives commented on her appearance. "She had enough gold dripping off her to put Elizabeth Taylor to shame," she said.

Ella - whose maiden name was Helen Russell - fell in love and became Mrs John McInnes in March, 1964. They had two children, Lorna and her little brother Kenneth. She lost a third child at birth. The couple later split and Ella and the children - Lorna was seven and Kenneth just three - went off to make a new and fresh start. She had fled hard-drinking McInnes and moved in with Ella's aunt Veitch Griffiths in a flat in Stonehouse's Main Street.

Now in this amazing phone call from Lorna, Ella was hearing an incredible story about her former husband. Lorna was telling her that police believed her dad was the notorious killer Bible John. Ella listened intently as her daughter told her detectives had applied for official permission to dig up her dad's remains. They wanted to exhume his body to do some sort of forensic examination, she said. It would all happen in the next few days. A team of police had been working on the Bible John case again and believed these tests could positively link dad and prove he was the killer. Ella's mind was in turmoil.

Her thoughts rushed back to the time in the 1960s when she had been interviewed by detectives about her husband at the height of the police hunt for Bible John. But that was more than a quarter of a century ago and she'd put all that to the furthest corner of her memory. She'd started a new life after all with a new husband, a new home and a new future.

"She just wants to put it all behind her," Rolfe Thornqvist told reporters who called afterwards.

"It is all history and no-one would involve her anyway. This is all in the past. They interviewed her at the time. If there had been any thought she knew anything they would have inquired into it. Obviously the police knew she had nothing to do with it."

ELLA THORNQVIST STANDS TODAY AS ONE OF BIBLE JOHN'S NEW VICTIMS.

She, like others, is faced with having to cope with the legacy of an evil chapter in Scottish criminal history. Bible John has returned to haunt not just John McInnes' family but the relatives and friends of three murder victims - Helen Puttock, Mima McDonald and Pat Docker.

Lorna Biggs, 32, who had called her mother from her home overlooking Lake Taupo, New Zealand, took time to come to terms with the shocking news of the renewed police activity back in Scotland. She told one reporter: "Oh God, it's all such a shock to me. I don't know anything that went on. To me it's all in the past. It's not so bad for me over here but this will really shock friends and people we know in Scotland."

Well-spoken Lorna, who moved to New Zealand five years ago, now shares a four-bedroomed house in central North Island with husband Dave and her children. The house is called Lochearn, the same name as her mum's five bedroomed holiday home in Lochearnhead, Perthshire. That house is just a few miles from fee-paying Morrison's Academy in Crieff, which Lorna and brother Kenneth attended.

Kenneth, 28, never really knew his father. "When he was part of my life I was only one year old. At the moment it's all a bit of a shock," he said after hearing the news. He lives in Thatcham, Berkshire, with his wife Lorraine, and when the news broke he didn't have the benefit of being thousands of miles away to distance himself from the glare of publicity. He was pictured covering his face as he moved from his car to his home, reluctant to speak to newspaper reporters.

Back in Lanarkshire, Stonehouse was turning a blind eye to the exhumation of John McInnes. They knew it was happening, but the locals couldn't bring themselves to go near the graveyard on that bitterly cold morning. "It's so hard to accept that old Mrs McInnes' rest is disturbed. It's the family left behind in the village that you have to feel sorry for in all this. How her son, Hector, and daughter, Etta, are coping I don't know. Hopefully they will find strength from somewhere and that will get them through this whole sorry episode," said a villager in hushed tones.

The brother and sister, who live near each other in the village, kept a dignified silence in the first few weeks after news broke of the exhumation.

Joan Beattie is very protective of her husband. She's been that way ever since he retired. Detective Superintendent Joe Beattie, the man who led the original Bible John hunt, has been dogged by ill-health for years. He lives with his wife in Bearsden on the outskirts of Glasgow. She fields his phone calls these days, telling most callers that he's resting and can't be disturbed. It's her way of looking after Joe. But a few months ago she opened her door to some very important callers - the new Strathclyde Police inquiry team investigating the Bible John murder mysteries. Joe spent many hours going over with them what he remembered about the original inquiry. As he progressed further in his police career the case had dominated his life. While he was director of detective training he spent hours talking about Bible John to his trainees. Another detective said: "Whenever a lecturer didn't turn up he would stand in. Inevitably he would bring up the subject. It appeared to be always on his mind - almost like an obsession."

The reopening of the Bible John inquiry after 27 years brings mixed feelings for Joe Beattie. The murder remains a mystery, but there has to be a secret torment that he may have missed Bible John when he was part of a police ID parade in the early days of the Helen Puttock murder investigation.

Memories of that same police ID parade must also prey on the mind of Jeannie Williams. Jeannie, the woman who came face to face with Bible John, the night he murdered her sister Helen, failed to pick him out from a line-up of suspects. Police have kept in constant touch with Jeannie over the years. Every time there was a new development, they were at her door, asking her questions and showing her pictures. When the first picture of John McInnes appeared in Scottish newspapers, police headed for Jeannie's Ayrshire home to show it to her. The nightmares, the questions and recriminations must have started all over again.

And for the families of Mima McDonald and Pat Docker the memories will never fade. Some have moved from Glasgow, and over the years have recalled these fateful nights out that left four youngsters without mothers. And as these youngsters grew up they could only rely on older relatives to paint a picture of the women they never got the chance to know properly.

David Puttock thinks about his mum's last minutes

on Earth to this day. He thinks about how she struggled to escape the clutches of her killer. David, 31, was just five when his mother Helen cheerily left for a night out at the Barrowland with his aunt Jeannie. He never saw his mother alive again.

At his home in Berkshire, indeed not far from where McInnes' son Kenneth lives, he revealed his inner feelings for the man who denied him and his brother Michael, now 28, the love, care and attention that only a mother can provide.

"I would have killed the murderer. I wanted to see him go through the same pain as mum did. I will never forget that he got away with this. I will never forgive him or his family. I just can't. What really hurts is that I didn't know my mum better. I didn't see how pretty she was, like dad describes her. I was too young to know her well.

"There's also anger because I didn't go to Scotland to try to find out more. The killer was still on the loose and I was doing nothing about it. I find that difficult to cope with. I want to know why she was murdered. Was it because he was sick or ill? It wouldn't make it easier to accept, but it is something I need to know. I wanted to see him alive because I wanted to find out why. But there was no arrest, no trial. He didn't exist. I can't let her memory go. I don't want her to be forgotten and I will tell my own children what happened to gran. On every birthday I think about her. I get distant and I think what it would be like if she was still here.

"Because of that bastard it is something I will never know."

George Puttock knelt in front of his wife Helen's gravestone for the first time since her funeral almost 27 years ago. At its base are inscribed two simple words:

"Always remembered." As he stared at that fading description he said: "I will always love Helen. She was just quite one of the most pretty girls I have ever met. She was full of life, full of fun. I will never forget her."

He will also never forget the morning he looked out of his front window and saw a police caravan at the end of his road. "I knew something had happened to Helen.

"I walked down the street towards the caravan and told a policeman my wife was missing.

"He asked me what she was wearing. When I told him he went and brought another policeman back. I will never forget him putting his hand on my shoulder and saying: 'I'M SORRY SON. YOUR WIFE'S BEEN MURDERED.

"I just felt numb. You lose all your senses."

Days after Helen's death, George, now 55, was quizzed as a suspect, but was quickly ruled out. Years on officers returned to ask him for DNA samples as part of the new investigation.

"The day they knocked on my door I was shaking. It all came flooding back, all the horror, so much pain. I knew the police had always thought I might be involved and this time I genuinely thought they had come for me. For years I couldn't understand why they hadn't trapped Helen's killer. For years I was convinced Helen had been killed by the Yorkshire Ripper. I had managed to link him to the place and the time.

"What everyone didn't seem to understand all these years is that I was dying inside, all these years of pain and anger. It was so bad that I never had the courage to visit her grave after the funeral."

The DNA results eliminated George from the suspects' list. He remembers how on that fateful night all these years ago he and Helen had argued before she left with Jeannie. George, an ex-Army sergeant hadn't wanted his wife to go dancing. He didn't think it was right for a married young mum to hit the town on her own. But Helen insisted and he relented. His concern for Helen's safety that night led him to give her the ten shillings for a taxi back home.

"That ten bob is the worst ten bob I have spent in my life. By midnight I was very worried she still wasn't back. Something just wasn't right. I knew she wouldn't do anything stupid because she loved the kids so much."

George's memory of these events are as clear today as if they had happened last week. The memory is etched on his mind and recounted as if he has relived each moment every day of the last 27 years. Ever since her murder George has had to cope with the cruel sex slurs and smears about Helen and the events of that last night. George, who remarried in 1973, jumps to defend Helen's memory. "People made her out to be a tart. That's what hurts most. I want people to know what Helen really was - a terrific mum and a vivacious girl."

George's concern about Helen's memory sparked a two-year legal fight against a TV firm when he claimed a programme branded her an easy good time girl and painted him as spineless and uncaring. The lawsuit took its toll, pushing him to the limit. And months after an out of court settlement was reached he collapsed when police asked him for the DNA.

The ordeal for George Puttock continues, exacerbated by the knowledge that the Bible John mystery goes on.

"I will hate the man who murdered Helen for the rest of my life.

"I WILL TAKE THAT HATE TO THE GRAVE."

# APPENDIX 1

## **CHRONOLOGY**

### April 21, 1921

John Irvine McInnes' parents Robert and
Elizabeth marry in Stonehouse.

### December 24, 1934

Barrowland Ballroom, Glasgow, opens for
the first time.

### September 10, 1938

John Irvine McInnes born 9 Holding, Sidehead
Road, Stonehouse.

### September 28, 1954

McInnes' father Robert dies.

### Summer, 1957

McInnes joins Army.

## July, 1959

McInnes discharged from the Army.

## March 16, 1964

John Irvine McInnes marries Helen - Ella - Russell at Muirkirk Parish Church, Ayrshire.

## December 2, 1964,

McInnes' daughter Doreen Lorna born.

## February 23, 1968

Pat Docker found murdered.

## May 29, 1968

McInnes' son Kenneth born.

## August 17, 1969.

Mima McDonald found murdered.

## October 31, 1969

Helen Puttock found murdered

## February 25, 1972

McInnes and wife Ella divorce at Ayr Sheriff Court.

## April 30, 1980

McInnes found dead at his mother's home in Stonehouse.

## September 18, 1987

McInnes' mother Elizabeth dies.

## January 27, 1996

Police announce they have asked for permission to exhume McInnes' body.

## February 1, 1996

McInnes' remains exhumed from his grave.

## July 4, 1996

----------------

The Lord Advocate says forensic tests fail to link McInnes with Puttock murder. He considers further circumstantial evidence.

# APPENDIX 2

## THEY SHAMED A NATION

THEIR names have brought shame to a proud nation.
They are Scotland's killers, the murder monsters whose
crimes are so sick they beggar belief. Even today, the
very mention of their names strike fear into the heart
young and old alike.

Serial murderers, razor killers and child sex monsters
with twisted minds, psychopaths and evil
schizophrenics - they all hold their place in a gory league
of evil. Other killers have earned their infamy through
the intense public interest in their cases. Some are there
simply because they are rotten to the core. Their names
will forever be written in blood in the country's
catalogues of crime. They have earned their place in the
Scottish history book of Hell.

### DENNIS NILSEN

Fraserburgh-born Nilsen carried out some of the most
despicable crimes known to man. It is believed he
murdered 15 young men at his two London homes
between 1979 and 1983, burying them beneath
floorboards and flushing their remains down sinks and
toilets. On November 4, 1983, an Old Bailey judge
recommended that he stay in jail for at least 25 years. For
12 hours and 26 minutes the jury deliberated over
whether he was guilty of murder - or manslaughter by
virtue of diminished responsibility. Finally they decided

he was sane, and by a 10-2 majority convicted him of six murders and two attempted murders. Homosexual Nilsen picked up young men and took them to his home in Cranley Gardens, Muswell Hill, North London. Detectives believe he killed at least 15 times. Nilsen has boasted that the figure is nearer 30. However only eight of his victims were positively identified. Nilsen cut up his victims, boiled their remains and then stuffed limbs in drains and sewers, showing no pity for the men he killed - or their families. He used butchery skills he learned in the Army to dissect the bodies before disposing of them. It was only after a Dyno-Rod worker had been called in to clear a blocked toilet that the crimes were uncovered. Complaints had been made by Nilsen's neighbours, and indeed the killer himself had written an indignant letter to the landlord's agents complaining about the drains and the unpleasant smell. The Dyno-Rod employee examined a manhole and found what he thought were human remains. When Nilsen arrived home from work that night he was quizzed by police. Detectives later found the remains of three bodies at the Cranley Gardens address and the remains of at least another eight bodies from his other home at Melrose Avenue, Cricklewood.

## ARCHIBALD HALL

Hall was the former Glasgow slum boy who killed four times and had a hand in a fifth. Smooth-talking Hall became known as The Mad Butler. Hall's trail of slaughter was fuelled by his desire to get rich quick. He wanted to live in luxury, and plotted to steal antiques from his wealthy bosses. He was jailed for life after slaughtering his brother, girlfriend and best friend - as well as his boss and his wife. In an amazing killing spree he firstly gunned down small-time crook David Wright, 30, of Dumfries. Eight weeks later he teamed up with his pal Michael Kitto to break into the London flat of Dorothy Scott-Elliot, 62, his former employer. When she disturbed them, they killed her, stuffed her body into their car and drove to Scotland with her ex-MP husband Walter as a hostage.

Dorothy was buried near Braco in Perthshire. Walter, who had been heavily drugged by the pair, was battered to death with a spade in Glen Affric. Hall's girlfriend Mary Coggie, who had been with the pair on the trip was killed with a poker back in London - after she'd made love to Hall on Mrs Scott-Elliot's mink coat. Then Hall turned on his brother Donald. He was killed because he knew too much. Hall and Kitto were caged for life at Edinburgh High Court in 1978 for murdering Mr Scott-Elliot and David Wright. In 1979, the Old Bailey heard Hall's confession to the murder of his brother and Mary Coggie. He was given life imprisonment. Kitto was jailed for 15 years for murdering Mary Coggie and the manslaughter of Donald Hall and Mrs Scott-Elliot.

# THOMAS CAMPBELL AND JOE STEELE

Campbell and Steele were jailed for life on October 10, 1984 for what became known as "The Ice Cream War Murders." The Doyle family from Ruchazie, Glasgow, were virtually wiped out when their flat was set on fire. James Doyle, 53, his sons James, 23, Andrew, 18, and 14-year-old Tony; daughter Christine Halleron, 25, and her 18-month-old baby Mark all died in the horror blaze. Three other victims eventually recovered. They were victims of a brutal war in which gangsters were trying to push ice cream sellers off their traditional patches.

Detectives believed that the ice cream vans were being used as a cover to sell drugs and stolen goods. Young Andrew Doyle, known as The Fat Boy, was hired as a minder to fend off the thugs. It led to him being blasted with a sawn-off shotgun as he worked in an ice cream van, although he escaped serious injury. After a campaign of terror against Andrew, the killers came to his family's top floor flat, poured petrol through the letterbox, threw a match - and six lives were painfully ended. Thomas "TC" Campbell was sentenced to life imprisonment with a recommendation that he serve at least 20 years. His henchman Joe Steele also got life. After Scotland's biggest mass murder trial, Lord Kincraig told them: "You are vicious and dangerous men." Campbell and Steele have protested their innocence since the day they were convicted. Steele has escaped from prison several times, once gluing himself to the gates of Buckingham Palace to publicise his fight. Campbell has carried out his protest from behind bars. Their campaign was rewarded in December 1996 when they were released pending appeal hearings.

## PETER MANUEL

Manuel was a mass murderer who earned the title of Scotland's most notorious killer. He even feigned madness in a desperate bid to escape the gallows. He showed the same dispassionate cunning that had claimed the lives of his seven victims. Manuel was convicted of the murders of 17-year-old Isabelle Cooke, 16-year-old Vivienne Watt and her mother and aunt and Peter and Doris Smart and their ten-year-old son Michael. The small-time robber who was named after three saints - Peter, Thomas, Anthony - turned to murder in a bid to gain the respect of Glasgow's ruthless underworld. It was generally accepted that he claimed five other lives. Police took Manuel to a field in the dark in a bid to trace the body of victim Isabelle Cooke. He said he couldn't find the location during the day. He had buried her in a shallow grave. After jumping over a ditch and walking across rough ground the trio came to a spot where the murderer pointed out some bricks and an ash bin where Isabelle's silver dancing shoes were discovered. After walking some distance the men came to another field which had been ploughed since he had buried his victim. Manuel walked about 15 to 20 yards from a tree then chillingly told the two detectives: "I think she is in there. I think I am standing on her."

He was sentenced to hang, but as his appointment with the hangman approached he put on a "mad act". He totally ignored his mother when she visited him. He kicked prison officers as they tried to dress him. He foamed at the mouth, twitching, pouting his lips and moving his head from side to side. He crouched on his bed with his legs crossed. And he refused to see doctors. For days on end the only words he would say was "chips". But the maniac failed to hoodwink three top psychiatrists and he was sent to the gallows in 1958, spending his last night alive playing cards and dominoes with his guards.

# ROBERT BLACK

Black, the Scots-born triple child sex killer, was given 10 life sentences in May 1994. And the judge said he should serve at least 35 years - until he is 82. And he added: "If possible you should be jailed for the whole of your life."

Black, 47, was convicted of murdering 11-year-old Susan Maxwell, five-year-old Caroline Hogg and 10-year-old Sarah Harper. As he was led away at the end of a 24 day trial he spoke his only words, sneering to two rows of 23 police officers: "Well done, boys."

Pervert Black was also suspected of killing at least 13 more innocent girls. The van driver prowled the length and breadth of the country searching for white-socked or bare-legged prey - just like Susan, Caroline and Sarah.

At the time of his sentencing in Newcastle he was already serving a life sentence for the kidnap and sex assault of a six-year-old girl in the Borders village of Stow. And it was his arrest there - by a fluke - that led to him being caged until he dies in prison.

Black was a reject and outcast from the moment he was conceived. He never knew his father or his mother. His background was a classic blueprint for the making of a child sex fiend. In his days at school in Kinlochleven, Argyll, he earned a reputation as a bully. And he was nicknamed Beasty and Smelly Bobby by classmates because of his strong body odour.

His reign of terror lasted for years and police believe his body count straddles Britain, possibly the Continent and even America. Scots police chief Hector Clark, who led the hunt for Black, spoke after the court verdicts. He said: "Black took the lives of three lovely little girls. It took me time to get over the relief of the verdicts. No matter how much experience you have, such moments still hit you. I don't care about Robert Black or what he says. He is a violent and evil man. I just hope there is not a second one like him out there."

## SHEILA GARVIE

Sheila Garvie was a young girl from a strict family background. She spent her teenage years on the Royal estate at Balmoral. She had tea with the Queen Mother and met the late King George IV. Her dad worked as a mason on the Highland estate. But 20 years later she stepped into the dock accused of murder. The victim was bludgeoned and shot to death on the night of May 14, 1968. The victim was Sheila's husband - wealthy, 35-year-old Maxwell Garvie. He was killed in an upstairs bedroom of his luxury farmhouse near Fordoun, Kincardineshire. Three months later Maxwell's rotting body was discovered in an underground tunnel near Cyrus, five miles north of Montrose.

Sheila Garvie, then 34, was the central figure in the dock the High Court in Aberdeen, in November, 1968.

Two men were accused with her - one, the handsome, bearded Brian Tevendale, a 23-year-old motor mechanic with whom she'd fallen in love. The other was 20-year-old Alan Peters.

The court hearing was dubbed the most sensational and baffling murder case in Scottish criminal history. Sensation followed sensation as the story of the events leading to the death of the big-spending Maxwell unfolded. Sheila Garvie sobbed as her mother collapsed in the witness box. The next day she was to listen as frail Edith Watson told how she betrayed her own daughter and her lover Tevendale to the police. For the three months between the night of his death and the day his body was found Maxwell - known for his daredevil stunts in his private plane - was simply thought missing.

But two days after he was killed, Sheila had confessed to her mum that he was not missing but dead.

Sheila was confident her mother would never divulge that secret. But she did. Had Mrs Watson remained tight-lipped Maxwell's disappearance would have remained a mystery.

During the trial Sheila, a mother of three, heard evidence from a long procession of prosecution witnesses. Among them was Trudy Birse, Tevendale's sister and Maxwell's former mistress. Trudy, the wife of a policeman, astounded the court with her tale of a bizarre sex foursome involving herself, Tevendale, and the Garvies. And Sheila was led from the dock when the jury was shown the skull of the murder victim. Sheila, an ex-Sunday School teacher, told how her marriage had turned into a nightmare of drinking, drugs and perverted sex. But Sheila Garvie was found guilty of murder on a majority verdict and sent to prison for life. Tevendale was also found guilty but the charge against Peters was found not proven. Sheila Garvie spent ten years in prison and afterwards claimed: "I had no hand in my husband's murder but I deserved my sentence because I failed to halt the tide of events which led to his death."

## THOMAS MCCULLOCH and ROBERT MONE

McCulloch and Mone were jailed for life in February, 1977, and labelled in court as "very dangerous men". The pair were inmates at the State Hospital at Carstairs in Lanarkshire.

McCulloch, then 26, admitted murdering nursing officer Neil McLellan, patient Ian Simpson, and police constable George Taylor in the previous November. Mone, 28, admitted murdering PC Taylor but denied killing the others - pleas accepted by the Crown.

The case shocked Scotland after it was revealed how the pair embarked on an orgy of killing. They had put into action an escape plan. When they were being taken to the recreation block, McCulloch attacked and killed the nursing officer and another patient.

The two climbed out of the hospital using a rope ladder and stopped a car outside. A police car arrived at the scene and the escapees began attacking PC Taylor. The pair hijacked the police car and were later recaptured in England.

At the High Court in Edinburgh it was revealed that the pair had been planning their escape for several months. They had assembled weapons, money, a map, clothes, the rope ladder, false papers and a false moustache.

The then Solicitor General Lord McCluskey said: "Both had been working in the joiners' workshop and there they had made the ladder and a knife. Mr McLellan must have tried to prevent the escape and McCulloch attacked him with an axe. Simpson must have joined in, perhaps to protect McLellan, but one does not know. Both men died of multiple head injuries."

Lord McCluskey said that, once outside the hospital

perimeter fence, the pair faked a road accident. Constable Taylor arrived at the scene and shone his torch in the face of one of his killers. He was immediately grabbed by the throat and the other arrived and attacked him with an axe.

Constable John Gillies tried to get help by sending a message over his radio. He then went to save his colleague but it was too late. The killers escaped in the police vehicle. Two men on their way to work noticed a crashed police vehicle. They drew up and saw a man in uniform waving him down. He asked for help and when the two workmen got out of their van they too were viciously attacked. Mone and McCulloch escaped in the van.

The pair crashed again near a farm in Biggar. They headed for the lonely farmhouse, occupied by Rennie Craig, his wife and four children. When Mr Craig answered the door he was confronted by the killers who were armed with an axe and a knife. They demanded his car and keys and went inside and ripped out the telephone. But they made a mistake - it was only an extension. This allowed Mr Craig to use the main phone to call the police, giving them a detailed description of the killers and his car.

After a 90mph chase a police car managed to get in front and forced the hijacked car into a slip road where it crashed into a roundabout. Undeterred, the pair tried to hijack another car but police arrived in time to overpower and disarm them. Passing sentence Lord Dunpark told the pair: "It is plainly no ordinary piece of mindless murder. You hatched a plot to leave Carstairs and you were determined to succeed even if you had to kill to do it."

# EPILOGUE

## THE SLAUGHTER OF THE INNOCENTS

THE country is still reeling from the actions of evil pervert Thomas Watt Hamilton. In just three fear-filled minutes he became Britain's worst mass murderer of the 20th century. The disgraced ex-Scout leader, armed with four guns, walked into a quiet primary school and sprayed bullets around the gym hall where a class of five and six-year-olds was exercising.

On the morning of Wednesday, March 13, 1996, 16 little boys and girls died in the carnage at Dunblane Primary School in Central Scotland. Their teacher Gwen Mayor, 45, was also murdered as she tried to protect the pupils. Other children survived the attack but were seriously injured. Hamilton, 43, turned the gun on himself, adding to the death toll.

The scenes over the next few hours were unbelievable as frantic parents rushed to the school to find out if their youngsters had been killed.

A local doctor treating the injured in a hospital 10 miles away discovered her own child had been shot dead.

The senseless slayings shocked the world. The Queen, Prime Minister and political leaders all over Europe sent messages of sympathy.

It was revealed that the gunman had spent months in an increasingly obsessive campaign against those he believed were persecuting him. He was forced to quit his links with the Scouts in the 70s after "inappropriate behaviour following a camp".

Hamilton had written to the Queen, claiming the

Scout Association had tarnished his name. He claimed there was a vendetta against him after he started running a number of groups for young boys.

Neighbours at his home in Kent Road, Stirling, spoke of dozens of pictures of little boys in his home. He also proudly showed neighbours a video of boys exercising.

Thomas Watt Hamilton's sick act ripped out the heart of a proud community.

Local MP Michael Forsyth, the Scottish Secretary of State, said: "It is the last place in the world where one would expect a tragedy of this kind."

The Shadow Secretary of State George Robertson MP who lives close to the school said the shootings were an act of "unspeakable brutality and evil".

That morning robbed Dunblane of its image as a picturesque gateway for visitors. Hamilton ensures its name will go on a roll-call of horror - always known as the scene of the massacre of schoolkids.

# SOURCE NOTES

THE following sources were used in the research and the writing of this book:

The Holy Bible, King James Version

Bloomsbury Dictionary Of Quotations

"Goodbye, Beloved Brethren" (1972)
by Norman Adams

"Bible John - Search for a Sadist" (1980)
by Charles Stoddart

"The Sadistic Murderer" (1970)
by Dr Robert P. Brittain

"The Missing" (1995) by Andrew O'Hagan

"Blood on the Thistle" (1992) by Douglas Skelton

"Scotland's Unsolved Mysteries of the Twentieth
Century" (1989) by Richard Wilson

and the following newspapers - The Sunday Mail, Daily
Record, Scottish Daily Mail, Scottish Daily Express,
Scotland On Sunday, Glasgow Evening Times, The
Herald, The Scotsman.*